House of Commons

Deputy Keeper of Public Records in Ireland

Thirty-First Report

House of Commons

Deputy Keeper of Public Records in Ireland
Thirty-First Report

ISBN/EAN: 9783742800039

Manufactured in Europe, USA, Canada, Australia, Japa

Cover: Foto ©Thomas Meinert / pixelio.de

Manufactured and distributed by brebook publishing software
(www.brebook.com)

House of Commons

Deputy Keeper of Public Records in Ireland

30 & 31 VICTORIA, CAP. 70, S. 24.

THE
THIRTY-FIRST REPORT

OF THE

DEPUTY KEEPER

OF THE

PUBLIC RECORDS AND KEEPER

OF THE

STATE PAPERS IN IRELAND.

[5TH MAY, 1899.]

Presented to both Houses of Parliament by Command of Her Majesty.

DUBLIN:
PRINTED FOR HER MAJESTY'S STATIONERY OFFICE,
BY ALEXANDER THOM & CO. (LIMITED).

And to be purchased, either directly or through any Bookseller, from
HODGES, FIGGIS and CO. (Limited), 104, Grafton street, Dublin; or
EYRE and SPOTTISWOODE, East Harding-street, Fleet-street, E.C., and
32, Abingdon-street, Westminster, S.W.; or
JOHN MENZIES & CO., 12, Hanover-street, Edinburgh, and
90, West Nile-street, Glasgow.

1899.

CONTENTS.

CHIEF SECRETARY'S OFFICE,

DUBLIN CASTLE.

31st *July*, 1890.

SIR,

I have to acknowledge the receipt of your letter of the 28th instant, forwarding, for submission to His Excellency the Lord Lieutenant, the Thirty-first Report of the Deputy Keeper of the Public Records and Keeper of the State Papers in Ireland.

I am, Sir,

Your obedient Servant,

(Signed),   D. HARREL.

The Deputy Keeper,
   Public Record Office,
      Four Courts.

THE THIRTY-FIRST REPORT

OF THE

DEPUTY KEEPER OF THE PUBLIC RECORDS AND KEEPER OF THE STATE PAPERS

IN IRELAND.

TO THE RIGHT HONORABLE THE EARL CADOGAN, K.G.,

LORD LIEUTENANT-GENERAL AND GENERAL GOVERNOR OF IRELAND

MAY IT PLEASE YOUR EXCELLENCY.

1. At Appendix I. of this Report is printed the emendations Appendix necessary to be made in the Addenda to the Index of the Act or Grant Books and Original Wills of the Diocese of Dublin 1272–1800, being Appendix IV. of my 26th Report, in consequence of the references to Marriage Licences between the periods 1672–1065 and 1713–1741 having been taken, in the absence of the original registers, from a transcript of a private Index. Since then the original books of Marriage Licences have been found, as stated in my last Report, and many mistakes were found to exist in the transcript. These are now corrected by printing the correct entries in cases where mistakes exist in the published Index.

2. I regret to have to report the death of Mr. J. C. Bailey, an experienced clerk in this Department, which occurred in the month of January. The vacancy has been filled by the appointment of Mr. J. F. Morrissey.

3. I have been approached by the Historical MSS. Commission, with a view to having MSS. committed to them, for the purpose of publication, deposited temporarily in the Strong Room for safe custody during examination and transcription by their Inspectors. I am very happy to have been able to meet the wishes of the Commission.

4. Permission was given by the Lords of H.M. Treasury to purchase some Records of the late Killaloe Diocesan Registry; also two lots at the auction of a portion of the library of the late Sir Thomas Phillipps, bart., which had apparently at one time formed portion of the Records of the Crown. Schedules are given at paragraphs 70 and 71 respectively.

5. The Title Book, 1638-1648, of the Diocese of Dublin, stated in the Introductory Note to the Appendix of my 20th Report to have been then in the custody of the Registrar of the diocese, has been transferred here (see paragraph 60).

State Paper Office.

6. The books and papers received from the Chief Secretary's Office during the year were of an unusually varied character. They included—

    1. The files of Letters received in that Office for the year 1868, occupying 71 cartons. Also the Registers of Letters received for 1886 to 1888, 10 large volumes.

    2. Sixty volumes of Letter Entry Books, as follows :—
        Government Letters, 1854-80.
        Irish Departmental Letters, 1850-76.
        Letter Book, "First Division," 1864-70.
        Irish Departmental and Country Letter Book, 1876-79.

    3. Papers of the Queen's Colleges Commission, 1884: Minute Books of Meetings, Minutes of Evidence, Letter Books, Correspondence and Draft Report, 5 cartons and 3 vols.

    4. Educational Endowments Commission, Minutes and Letter Books, 1879-81, 2 vols ; Papers and Returns, 1879-91, 14 cartons ; School Accounts, Parish of St. Bridget, Dublin, 1837-86, 8 vols.

    5. Abstracts of Poor Law Union Accounts, and Abstracts of Numbers of several classes of Paupers relieved in 1857, 4 portfolios.

    6. Boundary Commission, Ireland, under Redistribution of Seats Act, 1884 ; Minute Books, Registers of Letters, Minutes, Letters, Maps, and Draft Report, 1884-5.

    7. Commissioners of Ministers' Money, Tin Box containing Memoranda and Forms.

    8. Barrow Arterial Drainage, 1888, Maps, Plans, and Sections.

    9. Evicted Tenants Commission, 1892 ; Letters, Papers, and Books, 18 cartons, and 9 parcels.

7. The Searches made for the Chief Secretary's Office numbered 307, the largest number yet registered in one year.

8. The following, with the permission of the Lord Lieutenant or the Chief Secretary, were permitted to examine or obtain copies of State Papers : M. Felix Salomon of Leipzig, Mr. O'Connor Morris (on behalf of Lord Ashbourne), Colonel Lunham, and Mr. J. G. Swift MacNeill, M.P.

9. The letter files of 1838 received from the Chief Secretary's Office have been checked and placed in 40 carton boxes, numbered 3,411 to 3,458.

10. The arrangement of the Letters and Papers of the period 1760 to 1789, mentioned in last Report as having been commenced, has been completed, and a manuscript catalogue

prepared extending to nearly 700 pages. The collection as now arranged has been formed by bringing together the letters and papers of this period from the following collections in the State Paper Office already referred to in former reports, viz.:—

11. (a) "Miscellaneous State Papers" referred to by Old Official Index, arranged according to subjects (Rep. IV., p. 26, Rep. V., p. 31). This collection consists mainly of letters to the Irish Government from Public Departments or Officials in England and Ireland; classified in part according to the Department from which they came, and in part according to the subjects with which they deal. They include a continuation of the important series already transferred under the title of British Departmental Correspondence. The system of arrangement has been retained and has been supplemented by the addition of the letters and papers of this period found among the following:—

12. (b) "Miscellaneous State Papers," arranged chronologically, (Report V., p. 31). These papers were arranged in years in 1872, but the index then formed being of little practical value, all papers before 1790 have been withdrawn from it and amalgamated with this present collection.

13. (c) "Irish Departmental Correspondence." The majority of the papers of this small class were included in the collection of Papers earlier than 1760 mentioned in Rep. XXIX., s. 23, and Rep. XXX., s. 8. What remained of it has now been included in the present series.

14. (d) Miscellaneous Papers, 1760-1811, found by Sir B. Burke (see Rep. XIII., p. 14). Those prior to 1700 were included in the transfer of 1897; of the residue, those to 1780 are included in the present collection and in the Miscellaneous Papers which are to supplement it.

15. (e) The collection referred to in Sir B. Burke's VIII., (p 23), IX. (p. 17), and XVI. (p. 14) Reports. The papers of this collection commenced in 1779. Those from this date to 1789, which occupied 4 cartons, numbered 620/15, to 620/18, have been inserted in the collection now formed. These papers are not, as seems to be implied, included in the comprehensive index of this collection mentioned in Rep. XX., p. 26.

16. (f) Occasional documents for this period found during the general arrangement of the different collections.

17. Besides these Departmental Letters and Official Papers there are a number of Miscellaneous Letters and Papers, filling 5 or 6 cartons, for the same period and derived from the same sources. The arrangement and cataloguing of these also was commenced but could not be completed in 1898.

18. In addition to the work in arranging and cataloguing these Official Letters and Papers, the following classes have been cleaned, examined, arranged, made up in brown paper parcels, and labelled, and entered up:—

Letters and Papers of Commissioners of Customs, 1790-1831.

Letters and Papers of Commissioners of Excise, 1797-1835.

Constabulary, Letters of Major Miller, Inspector-General of the Munster Constabulary, 1829-30.

Other Constabulary Returns and Papers, 1828–36.
Crown Solicitors' Accounts, 1801–35.
Relief Commission Papers, 1843–47.
Land Commission, 1844: Papers, 1843–44.
The following were transferred to the Record Office during the year :—

Departmental Letters and Official Papers, 1760–80.
Land Commission, 1844 Correspondence, Returns, and Minutes of Evidence and Proceedings.

10. The DEPARTMENTAL LETTERS AND OFFICIAL PAPERS, as has been observed, are arranged according to Departments and subjects. A list of the Heads of this collection was given in the 4th Report, D.K.R., pp. 24–5. As the papers under many of the heads in that list do not commence until after the period covered by the collection now transferred, it may not be amiss to give a list of the heads under which the papers now transferred are grouped. In this the more important or more numerously represented heads are given in capitals :—

Accounts, 1763–80; Addresses, 1778–80; Admiralty, 1760–82; Annuities, 1778–89; Banks, 1782–89; Barracks and Public Works Commissioners, 1760–89; Chief Secretary's Office, 1777–85; Commander of the Forces, 1777–70; Convicts, 1762–89; Council Office, London, 1762–82; COUNCIL OFFICE, Dublin, 1760–89; Courts of Law and Equity, 1779–89; Crown Lands, 1763–87; Crown Solicitor, 1779–89; Currency, 1768–89; Customs Commissioners, 1772–89; Dublin Castle, 1763–84; Dublin Paving Board, 1787–88; Dublin Police, 1784–80; Dublin Quay Walls, 1784–89; Dublin Wide Street Commissioners, 1777–84; Ecclesiastical, 1759–80; Education, 1786–84; Excise Office, 1772–89; Fairs and Markets, 1760–78; Fisheries, 1774–83; Geneva Colony and New Geneva, 1783–89; House of Industry, 1771–89; HOME OFFICE, 1760–89; IRISH OFFICE, 1760–85; Inland Navigation, 1772–88; Knights of St. Patrick, 1783; Law Opinions, 1772–87; Light Houses, 1768–89; Linen Board, 1774–85; Lotteries, 1780–89; LORD LIEUTENANT, 1760–89; Magistracy, 1787–89; Military Miscellaneous, 1759–89; Naval, 1770–88; PARLIAMENT, 1763–89; Patents, 1728–89, Peerage Claims, 1772–88; Phoenix Park, 1762–89; Post Office, 1762–89; Prisons, 1765–89; Quarantine, 1760–89; Quarter Sessions, 1783; REVENUE COMMISSIONERS, 1760–89; Roman Catholic Priests, 1782–87; Roman Catholic Oaths, 1770–87; Secret Service, 1787–83; Sheriffs, 1771–89; Smuggling, 1777–86; Stamp Office, 1773–89; STATE OF COUNTRY, 1760–89; Stationery and King's Printer, 1763–86; Surveys, 1786–89; Trade and Manufactures, 1776–89; TREASURY, 1760–89; Volunteer, 1778–87; Ulster King of Arms, 1780–88; War Office, 1760–79.

20. This collection of Departmental Letters may be regarded as forming the continuation of the important class of British Departmental Correspondence transferred in 1894. The letters from the principal Government Departments have generally been put up with considerable regularity, yet frequent gaps occur in every series. Appendix II. contains a few notes by Mr. James Mills of this collection.

Appendix II.

TRANSFERS.

There have been transferred and deposited here during the past year Records from the under-mentioned Courts and Offices as set out in the following lists :—

21. From the Record and Writ Office, Chancery :—

Records	Date	Vols.	Prels.
Affidavits, ...	1877	64	—
„ Index to, ...	"	1	—
Answers, ...	"	1	—
Appearances, ...	1876-7	2	—
Awards, Piers and Harbours, ...	1877	—	1
Bill Book, ...	"	3	—
Bills, ...	"	8	—
„ and Answers, Index to, ...	"	1	—
Certificates, Chief Clerks', ...	"	8	—
„ Lower Scale, ...	"	1	—
Comments, ...	"	1	—
Crown Lands, Conveyances of, ...	"	—	1
Depositions and Evidences, ...	"	1	—
Dismantling Deeds Rolls, ...	"	—	1
Draft Books, ...	1876-7	2	—
Ecclesiastical Deeds Enrolled, ...	1877	1	—
Fiants, ...	1874-8	1	—
Maps, Drainage, ...	1877	—	1
Motions, Landed Estates Court, ...	"	5	—
Notices, ...	"	10	—
Orders, Lord Chancellor's Court and Chamber, .	"	2	—
„ Masters'	1871-7	1	—
„ Rolls Court and Chamber, . . .	1877	2	—
„ Vice-Chancellor's Court and Chamber, .	"	3	—
„ General Index to, ...	"	1	—
„ and Notices of Motions and Miscellaneous, .	"	3	—
„ „ (L. E. C.) Register of Service of, .	1876-7	8	—
Patent Roll, ...	1877	—	1
Petitions, ...	"	2	—
„ Index to, ...	"	1	—
„ of Appeal and Answers thereto, . . .	"	1	—
Receivers' Accounts, ...	"	7	—
Recognisance Roll, ...	"	—	1
Recognisances, ...	"	—	1

Record and Writ Office, Chancery—continued.

Records.	Date.	Vols.	Pris.
Replications, Traversing Notes and Demurrers, ...	1865-77	1	—
Solicitors, Affidavits and Certificates for Admission of, . . .	1876-7	1	—
Solicitors' Apprentices, Indentures of.	1870-6	1	—
„ „ Affidavits of perfection of Indentures, .	1876-7	1	—
Summonses, Originating Administration, ...	1877	1	—
„ „ „ Index to, . . .	„	1	—

22. From the Land Judges Court, Chancery :—

Records.	Date.	Vols.	Pris.
Affidavits, ...	1876-77	80	—
„ Alphabetical List of, ...	„	1	—
„ Numerical List of, ...	„	1	—
Allnut's Irish Land Schedules, ...	1850-1873	1	—
Appearance Books, ...	1875-1877	3	—
Bespeak Book (Solicitors), ...	1876-1877	1	—
„ Books for Copies of Documents, ...	1859-1865	10	—
„ „ Record and Affidavit, ...	1876-1877	3	—
Bidding Book, Earl of Belmore's Estate, . . .	1851	1	—
Building Leases, Copies of, ...	1876-1877	—	1
„ „ Petitions for, ...	1877	—	1
Cash Balancing Books, ...	1876-1877	1	—
„ Bank, ...	1885	1	—
„ Receipt Book, ...	1876-1877	1	—
Claims, ...	1877	—	1
Conveyance Receipt Book, ...	1875-1876	1	—
Conveyances, Copies of, ...	1875-1877	—	6
„ Record of, ...	1871-1877	8	—
Declarations of Title, ...	1872-1877	—	1
Landlord and Tenant Act (1870) Charging Orders, .	1871-1877	—	1
„ „ „ Statement, . . .	1877	—	1
Miscellaneous Documents, ...	1876, 1876, and 1877	—	3
Notices to Tenants, ...	1871-1877	—	4
„ „ Objections to, . . .	1877-1878	—	1
Order Book (Absolute), ...	1876-1877	1	—
„ Books (Chief Clerk's), . . .	1876-1876	2	—
„ „ (Conditional), . .	1876-1877	8	—
„ „ (Miscellaneous), .	1876-1877	2	—

LAND JUDGES COURT, CHANCERY—*continued.*

Records.	Date.	Vols.	Pcis.
Orders Absolute, Directions for Amending, ...	1874-1877	1	—
,, Miscellaneous, Index to (Registrar's Office), . . .	1873-1874	1	—
,, ,, ,, (Flanagan), ...	1873-73	1	—
,, ,, ,, (Lynch), ...	—	1	—
,, Partition, ...	1862-77	—	1
Paymasters' Certificates, ...	1876-77	—	1
Petitions, ...	1877	7	—
,, Index to, ...	1844-9	1	—
,, ...	1873-77	2	—
Postings for Sale, Indexes to, ...	1853-69	2	—
Record of Proceedings, ...	1875-77	2	—
Rentals, Estate of the Countess of Kingston, . . .	1871	1	—
,, (Declaration of Title Cases), ...	1860-75	1	—
,, (Flanagan), ...	1877	2	—
,, Miscellaneous, ...	1858-77	—	3
,, MS., ...	1869-74	1	—
,, (Ormsby), ...	1877	8	—
,, (Registrar's Office), ...	1876-77	4	—
Sale Book, General, ...	1869-75	1	—
,, Books, Court, ...	1871-77 one entry for 1878	2	—
Sales, Private Proposals for, ...	1877	—	1
,, Provincial, Rentals with Auctioneers' Affidavits, . .	,,	—	1
Schedules of Incumbrances, Draft Final, ...	,,	2	—
,, ,, (Flanagan), . . .	,,	1	—
,, ,, (Ormsby), . . .	,,	8	—
,, ,, Objections to, Final, . . .	,,	1	—
Scrivenery Account Book, ...	1864-65	1	—
Solicitors' Licenses, Register of, ...	1877	1	—
,, Registry Books, ...	1869-69	9	—

23. From the Office of Registrar in Lunacy:—

Records.	Date.	Vols.	Pcis.
Accounts, ...	1877	1	—
Affidavits, ...	,,	1	—
Petitions and Reports, ...	,,	2	—

24. From the Vice-Chancellor's Office :—

Records.	Date.	Vols.	Pmts.
Cause Papers, ...	1857-77	—	3
Claim Book, ...	1868-73	1	—
Direction Books.	1860-77	6	—
Document Receipt Book, ...	1873-77	1	—
Note Books (Chief Clerk's), ...	1853-76	3	—
„ (Junior Clerks')	1862-77	13	—
Petition Book (Summary), ...	1857-1880	1	—
Proceedings, Registers of, ...	1867-76	6	—

25. From the Queen's Bench Division :—

Records.	Date.	Vols.	Prts.
Affidavit Books, ...	1857	1	—
Affidavits, ...	„	3	—
„ Judgment Mortgage, ...	„	2	—
„ „ „ Book, ...	1854-67	1	—
Bills of Sale, ...	1857	1	—
„ „ Index to, ...	1866-7	1	—
Cause Books, ...	1857	6	—
„ „ Indexes to, ...	„	2	—
Certificates of Taxed Costs, ...	1853-7	1	—
Certiorari, Writs of, ...	1859-7	1	—
Consent Book, ...	1876-87	1	—
Consents, ...	1856-7	1	—
Court Books, ...	1857	6	—
Executions, ...	„	1	—
Judgment Books, ...	„	1	—
Judgments, ...	„	13	—
„ Certificates of, under Judgment Extension Act. 1868,	1869-88	1	—
Masters' Reports, ...	1873-87	1	—
Memorials of Assignments of Judgments	1873-87	1	—
Pleadings, ...	1857	3	—
„ Miscellaneous, taken off File pursuant to Orders, .	1878-88	1	—
Praecipe Book, ...	1857	1	—
Praecipes, ...	„	6	—
Recognizances, ...	1854-67 and one of 1881	1	—
Registrars' Certificates, ...	1878-87	1	—
Returned Writs Book, ...	„	1	—

QUEEN'S BENCH DIVISION—*continued*.

Records.	Date.	Vols.	Prefs.
Rule Books, ...	1887	5	—
Satisfaction Book, ...	1871–87	1	—
Satisfactions, ...	1884–7	1	—
Warrants, ...	1887	4	—
Writs of Summons, ...	.	10	—

20. From the Queen's Bench (late Common Pleas) Division :—

Records.	Date.	Vols.	Prefs.
Affidavit Book, ...	1887	1	—
Affidavits, ...	.	5	—
„ Judgment Mortgage, ...	.	1	—
„ „ „ Index to, ...	1882–7	1	—
Award Book, ...	1864–67	1	—
Case Stated for Opinion of Court, ...	1885	—	1
Cause Books, ...	1887	2	—
„ „ Index to, ...	. .	1	—
Clerk of Rules Book, ...	1878	1	—
Conveits, ...	1887	1	—
„ and Awards, ...	1870–87	1	—
Court Books, ...	1887	7	—
Execution Book, ...	1882–7	1	—
Judgment Book, ...	1887	1	—
Judgments, ...	.	15	—
„ English (under Judgment Extension Act, 1868), .	1881–86	2	—
„ on Conveits and Warrants, ...	1882–80	1	—
Memorials of Assignments of Judgments, ...	1877–87	1	—
„ „ „ Index to, . . .	1880–87	1	—
Orders, Chamber, ...	1879–88	5	—
Pleadings, ...	1887	4	—
Precipes, ...	.	2	—
„ Index to, ...	.	1	—
Registrars' Certificates, ...	1884–87	1	—
Returned Writs, ...	1887	1	—
Rule Books, ...	.	3	—
Satisfaction Book, ...	1886–87	1	—
Satisfactions, ...	1882–7	1	—
Side Bar Rule Book, ...	1887	1	—
Writs of Summons, ...	1887	13	—

27. From the Queen's Bench (late Exchequer) Division :—

Records.	Date.	Vols.	Prels.
Affidavit Book, ...	1857	1	—
Affidavits, ...	"	3	—
Oaths Books, ...	"	6	—
" " Index to, ...	"	1	—
Court Books, ...	"	4	—
Judgment Book, ...	"	1	—
Judgments, ...	"	10	—
" on Cognovit, ...	1856, 1857	8	—
Pleadings, ...	1857	9	—
Precipes, ...	"	8	—
Rule Books, ...	1856, 1857	8	—
Side Bar Order Book, ...	1853-7	1	—
Writs of Summons, ...	1856, 1857	18	—

28. From the Queen's Bench Division (Bankruptcy) :—

Records.	Date.	Vols.	Prels.
Day List Book (Chief Registrar's and Chief Clerk's), . . .	1877	1	—
Debtors' Summonses, ...	"	8	—
Declarations of Poverty, ...	1874-7	1	—
" by Debtors in Prison. Register of,	1873-7	1	—
Files (Arrangement), ...	1877	—	6
" (Bankruptcy), ...	"	—	6
Insolvency. Declarations of, ...	"	—	1
Note Books, Chief Clerks', ...	"	2	..
" " Registrars', ...	1876-7	2	—
" " Registrars', ...	1877	6	—
Sittings Book (Court), ...	"	1	—

29. From the Queen's Bench Division (Probate), Principal Registry :—

Records.	Date.	Vols.	Prels.
Affidavits leading to Citations, . . .	1877	—	2
" of Scripts, ...	"	—	1
Bonds and Papers leading to Grants, . .	"	—	21
Calendar, ...	"	1	—
Caveat Book, ...	"	1	—
Contentious Papers, ...	"	—	6

QUEEN'S BENCH DIVISION (PROBATE)—continued.

Records.	Date.	Vols.	Prels.
Day Book, ...	1876-7	1	—
Grant Books, ...	1877	4	—
„ „ (District), ...	„	8	—
Matrimonial Cause Papers, ...	1872-7	—	1
Records (bound), ...	1877	1	—
Rule Book (Court), ...	„	1	—
„ „ Registrar's, ...	„	1	—
Schedules, ...	„	8	—
Side Bar Order Book, ...	1876-7	1	—
Stamp Office Certificates, ...	1877	—	8
Taxed Costs, ...	„	2	—
Will Books, ...	„	3	—
„ „ (District), ...	„	4	—
Wills, ...	„	—	41
„ Unproved, ...	„	—	1
Warning Certificate Book, ...	1875-6	1	—

30. From the ARMAGH District Probate Registry :—

Records.	Date.	Vols.	Prels.
Application Book, ...	1871-77	1	—
Caveats	1868-77	1	—
Caveats, ...	1877	—	1
Grant Books (Intestacies), ...	1872-77	1	—
„ „ (Probates), ...	1873-77	1	—
„ „ (Wills annexed), ...	1872-77	1	—
Index to Wills, &c., ...	1858-1877	1	—
Wills and Papers leading to Grants of Probate and Administration,	1877	—	16
Wills (Unproved), ...	„	—	1

31. From the BALLINA District Probate Registry :—

Records.	Date.	Vols.	Prels.
Wills and Papers leading to Grants of Probate and Administration,	1877	—	2

32. From the BELFAST District Probate Registry :—

Records.	Date.	Vols.	Prch.
Caveats, ...	1877	..	1
Grant Book (Probates), ...	1876-77	1	—
Renunciations, ...	1877	—	1
Wills and Papers leading to Grants of Probate and Administration,	„	—	9
Wills (Unproved), ...	„	—	1

33. From the CAVAN District Probate Registry :—

Records.	Date.	Vols.	Prch.
Applications, ...	1877	—	1
Caveat, ...	„	—	1
Wills and Papers leading to Grants of Probate and Administration,	„	—	1
Wills (Unproved), ...	„	—	1

34. From the CORK District Probate Registry :—

Records.	Date.	Vols.	Prch.
Grant Books (Intestates), ...	1876-77	1	—
„ „ (Probates), ...	1876-77	2	—
„ „ (Wills Annexed), ...	1876-77	1	—
Wills and Papers leading to Grants of Probate and Administration,	1877	—	4

35. From the KILKENNY District Probate Registry :—

Records.	Date.	Vols.	Prch.
Wills and Papers leading to Grants of Probate and Administration,	1877	—	1

36. From the LIMERICK District Probate Registry :—

Records.	Date.	Vols.	Prch.
Grant Book (Probates), ...	1876-77	1	—
Wills and Papers leading to Grants of Probate and Administration,	1877	—	1

37. From the LONDONDERRY District Probate Registry :—

Records	Date.	Vols.	Pris.
Grant Books (Intestales), ...	1873-77	1	—
„ „ (Probates, ...	1876-77	1	—
„ „ (Wills annexed), ...	1863-77	1	—
Wills and Papers leading to Grants of Probate and Adminis-tration.	1877	—	1

38. From the MULLINGAR District Probate Registry :—

Records.	Date.	Vols.	Pris.
Grant Books (Intestates), ...	1869 77	1	.
„ „ (Probates), ...	1878-77	1	—
„ „ (Wills annexed), ...	1869-77	1	—
Wills and Papers leading to Grants of Probate and Adminis-tration.	1877	—	1

39. From the TUAM District Probate Registry :—

Records	Date.	Vols.	Pris.
Caveats, ...	1877	—	1
Wills and Papers leading to Grants of Probate and Adminis-tration.	„	—	1

40. From the WATERFORD District Probate Registry :—

Records.	Date.	Vols.	Pris.
Grant Books (Probates), ...	1873-77	1	—
„ „ (Wills annexed), ...	1873 -77	1	—
Wills and Papers leading to Grants of Probate and Adminis-tration.	1877	—	1

41. From the Office of the Registrar of Judgments :—

Records.	Date.	Vols.	Pris.
Memorandums of Judgments obtained after 1850, . . .	1871-77	48	—
„ „ Burketry of Judgments and other incum-brances affecting Real Estate	„	11	—
Memorandums of Satisfaction, ...	„	4	—
Register of Judgments, Revivals, Decrees, Rules, and Orders after 15th July, 1850	1874-78	16	—
Requisitions for Searches, ...	1871-77	24	—

42. From the State Paper Office :—

Records.	Date.	Vols.	Prels.
Land Commission, 1844 :—			
Chancery Returns, ...	1841-3	—	1
" " rejected, ...	—	—	1
Circulars and Correspondence, ...	1844-5	—	1
Civil Bill Ejectments, Summary of Returns of, . . .	1839-45	—	1
Complaints, Register of, ...	1844-5	1	—
Correspondence, Register of Letters received, . . .	1843-4	2	—
County Cess, Statement of, ...	1841-4	—	1
" " Summary of, ...	1841-4	—	1
" " Return of, ...	1775-1846	—	1
Ejectments at Sessions, Return of, ...	1838-44	—	1
Ejectments, Returns of :—			
Court of Queen's Bench, ...	1841	—	1
" Common Pleas, ...	1841-3	—	1
" Exchequer, ...	"	—	1
Estates on which Receivers have been appointed, Return of, .	1834-43	—	1
Griffith's Notes on Unimproved Land, Returns and Statements,	1839-45	—	1
Leases, Copies of, ...	1829-45	—	1
Letters Despatched, Register of, ...	1844-5	1	—
" Received, ...	1843-5	—	4
Minutes of Evidence, Notes of the Examinations of Witnesses,	1843-5	1,183	—
Minutes of Proceedings :—			
Names of Witnesses and Correspondence :—			
County Antrim, ...	1843-4		
" Armagh, ...	"		
" Carlow, ...	"		
" Cavan, ...	"		
" Clare, ...	"		
" Cork, ...	"		
" Donegal	"		
" Down, ...	"		
" Dublin, ...	"		
" Fermanagh, ...	"	13	—
" Galway, ...	"		
" Kerry, ...	"		
" Kildare, ...	"		
" Kilkenny, ...	"		
" King's, ...	"		
" Leitrim, ...	"		
" Limerick, ...	"		

State Paper Office—continued.

Records.	Date.	Vols.	Price.
Land Commission, 1844:—			
Minutes of Proceedings:—			
Names of Witnesses and Correspondence:—			
County Londonderry.	1843-4		
„ Longford, ...	„		
„ Louth, ...	„		
„ Mayo, ...	„		
„ Monaghan, ...	„		
„ Queen's, ...	„		
„ Roscommon, ...	„	13	—
„ Sligo, ...	„		
„ Tipperary, ...	„		
„ Tyrone, ...	„		
„ Waterford, ...	„		
„ Westmeath, ...	„		
„ Wexford, ...	„		
„ Wicklow.			
Papers, Mixed and Miscellaneous unregistered, ...	1843-45	—	1
Petitions and Union Returns, ...	1843-4	—	1
Statements of Individual Cases of Grievances, ...	1844	60	—
Stationary Order Books, ...	1843-4	2	—
Witnesses, Alphabetical Arrangement of, ...	1843-6	—	1
„ List of, ...	1844-5	—	1
„ Numerical List of, ...	„	—	1
Departmental Letters and Official Papers:—			
Accounts, ...	1763-89		
Addresses, ...	1776-89		
Admiralty, ...	1780-83		
Annuities, ...	1778-83	—	1
Banks, ...	1782-89		
Barracks and Public Works Commissioners, ...	1780-89		
Chief Secretary's Office, ...	1777-89		
Commander of the Forces, ...	1787-9		
Convicts, ...	1782-89	—	1
Council Office, London, ...	1763-89		
„ „ Ireland, ...	1789-89	—	2
Courts of Law and Equity, ...	1778-89		
Crown Lands, ...	1783-87		
„ Solicitor, ...	1778-89	—	1
Currency, ...	1789-89		
Customs Commissioners, ...	1773-89		

STATE PAPER OFFICE—*continued.*

Records.	Date.	Vols.	Prels.
Official Letters and Papers:—			
Dublin Castle, ...	1763–84		
„ Paving Board, ...	1787–8		
„ Police, ...	1784–9	—	1
Dublin Quay Walls, ...	1785–9		
„ Wide Street Commissioners, . . .	1777–84		
Ecclesiastical, ...	1759–69	—	1
Education, ...	1759–8		
Excise Office, ...	1772–89		
Fairs and Markets, ...	1760–76		
Fisheries, ...	1774–86	—	1
Geneva Colony and New Geneva, . .	1753–89		
House of Industry, ...	1771–89		
Home Office, ...	1780–89	—	4
Inland Navigation, ...	1778–83	—	1
Irish Office, ...	1780–85	—	2
Knights of Saint Patrick, ...	1783		
Law Opinions, ...	1778–87	—	1
Light Houses, ...	1763–89		
Linen Board, ...	1774–85		
Lord Lieutenant, ...	1760–89	—	1
Lotteries, ...	1780–89	—	1
Magistracy, ...	1787–9		
Military Miscellaneous, ...	1759–69	—	1
Naval, ...	1770–85		
Parliament, ...	1763–89	—	4
Patents, ...	1785–89	—	2
Peerage Claims, ...	1778–82		
Phœnix Park, ...	1765–89		
Post-Office, ...	1785–79		
Prisons, ...	1786–89	—	1
Quarantine, ...	1760–89		
Quarter Sessions, ...	1783		
Revenue Commissioners, . . .	1760–89	—	1
Roman Catholic Oaths, . . .	1770–87		
„ „ Priests, . . .	1783–7	—	1
Secret Service, ...	1767–68		
Sheriffs, ...	1771–89		
Smuggling, ...	1777–85		
Stamp Office, ...	1773–89	—	1
State of Country, ...	1760–89		

STATE PAPER OFFICE—*continued*.

Records.	Date.	Vols.	Prels.
Official Letters and Papers :—			
Stationery and King's Printer, ...	1769-20	} —	1
Surveys, ...	1785-20		
Trade and Manufactures, ...	1778-80	—	1
Treasury, ...	1780-80	—	1
Ulster King of Arms, ...	1780-8		
Volunteers, ...	1778-87	} —	1
War Office, ...	1760-71		

43. From the Quit Rent Office :—

Records.	Date.	Vols.	Prels.
Twopenny Books, ...	1817-8	14	—

44. From the Crown and Peace Office of the county of Armagh :—

Records.	Date.	Vols.	Prels.
Appeals to Assizes, ...	1877	—	1
Civil Bill Books, ...	1876-7	9	—
Coroners' Inquests, ...	1876-7	—	1
Crown Files at Assizes, ...	1877	—	1
„ „ „ Quarter Sessions, ...	„	—	1
Deputy Lieutenant's Qualification, ...	1876	—	1
Ejectment Book (Chairman's), ...	1876-7	1	—
Jurors' Lists, ...	1877	—	1
Presentment Books, ...	„	2	—
Presentments, ...	„	—	1
Probate (Civil Bill) Book, ...	1860-77	1	—
„ Papers, ...	1873-7	—	1
Proclamations, ...	1877	—	1
Query Books, ...	„	4	—
Renewal Affidavits, ...	„	—	1
Spirit Licence Lists, ...	1876	—	1
„ „ Register, ...	1876-7	1	—
Summons and Plaints, ...	1876-7	—	1
Voters' Lists, Claims, and Objections, ...	1877	—	1

45. From the Crown and Peace Office of the county of Carlow:—

Records.	Date.	Vols.	Pcls.
Coroners' Inquests, ...	1876-7	—	1
Crown Files at Assizes.	1877	—	1
„ and Civil Files at Quarter Sessions, ...	„	—	1

46. From the Crown and Peace Office of the county of Cavan:—

Records.	Date.	Vols.	Pcls.
Civil Bill Book,.	1876-7	1	—
„ „ Papers, ...	1877	—	1
Coroners' Inquests, ...	1876-7	—	1
Crown Files at Assizes, ...	1877	—	1
„ „ „ Quarter Sessions, ...	„	—	1
Jurors' Books, ...	„	2	—
„ Lists, ...	„	—	1
Landlord and Tenant (1870) Act, Papers, . . .	„	—	1
Maps, Plans, Awards, &c., ...	„	—	1
Presentment (Abstract) Book, ...	„	1	—
„ „ Books, ...	„	—	1
Probate Papers, ...	„	—	1
Process Servers' Books, ...	1873-7	2	—
Publicans' Licence Notices, ...	1877	—	1
„ „ Register, ...	„	1	—
Sessions (Petty) District Papers, ...	1876-7	—	1
Voters' Lists, Claims, &c., ...	1877	—	1
„ Registers, ...	„	—	1

47. From the Crown and Peace Office of the county of Down:—

Records.	Date.	Vols.	Pcls.
Civil Bill Books, ...	1876-7	1	—
Crown Files at Assizes, ...	„	—	1
„ „ „ Quarter Sessions, . . .	1877	—	1
Fishery Papers, ...	1876-7	—	1
Grand Jury Bill Book, ...	1863-78	1	—

OP THE PUBLIC RECORDS IN IRELAND. 23

CROWN AND PEACE OFFICE, COUNTY OF DOWN—*continued.*

Records.	Date.	Vols.	Prels.
Jurors' Lists,	1877	—	1
Landlord and Tenant (1870) Act: Papers,	„	—	1
Magistrates' and Cess Payers' Declarations,	1876-7	—	1
Maps, Plans, Awards, &c.,	1876-7	—	2
Presentment Books,	1877	8	—
Presentments,	„	—	2
Query Books,	„	2	—
Renewal Affidavits,	„	—	1
Voters' Registers and Lists,	„	—	1

48. From the Crown Office of the county and of the county of the city of Dublin :—

Records.	Date.	Vols.	Prels.
Crown Files at Assizes,	1877	—	2

49. From the Peace Office of the county of Dublin :—

Records.	Date.	Vols.	Prels.
Appeals from Quarter Sessions,	1877	—	1
„ to „	„	—	1
Jurors' Petitions against Fines,	„	—	1
Jury Panels and Precepts,	„	—	1
Magistrates' and Cess Payers' Lists,	„	—	1
Maps, Plans, Awards, &c.,	„	—	6
Publicans' License Notices,	„	—	1
Renewal Affidavits,	„	—	1
Summons and Plaint,	„	—	1
Voters' Registers and Lists,	„	10	—

50. From the Peace Office of the county of the city of Dublin :—

Records.	Date.	Vols.	Pels.
Convictions and Appeals.	1877	—	1
Criminal Return, ...	"	—	—
Crown Files at Quarter Sessions, ...	"	—	1
Jurors' Lists Books, ...	"	4	—
" Petitions to remit Fines, ...	"	—	1
Maps, Plans, Awards, &c., ...	1875–7	—	4
Presentment Book (Schedule of Applications), ...	1877	1	—
Publicans' Licence Application Book, ...	1884–6	1	—
" " Notices, ...	1875–7	—	1
Voters' Lists, ...	1877	18	—

51. From the Crown and Peace Office of the county of Fermanagh :—

Records.	Date.	Vols.	Pels.
Appeals to Assizes, ...	1877	—	1
Civil Bill Papers, ...	"	—	1
Constable's (High) Appointment, ...	"	—	1
Crown Files at Quarter Sessions, ...	"	—	1
Explosives Act (1875) Papers, ...	1875	—	1
Presentment (Abstract) Book, ...	1877	1	—
Process Servers' Books, ...	1871–77	4	—

52. From the Crown and Peace Office of the county of Kerry :—

Records.	Date.	Vols.	Pels.
Appeals to Assizes, ...	1877	—	1
Civil Bill Books, ...	1876–7	6	—
" " Papers, ...	1877	—	1
Crown Book at Assizes, ...	"	1	—
" Files "	"	—	1
" " Quarter Sessions, ...	"	—	1
Ejectment Book (Tralee), ...	1876–7	1	—

CROWN AND PEACE OFFICE, COUNTY OF KERRY--*continued.*

Records.	Date.	Vols.	Pris.
Fishery Papers,	1877	—	1
Jurors' Books,	"	2	—
" Lists,	"	"	1
Landlord and Tenant (1870) Act: Court Book,	"	1	—
" " " Papers,	"	"	1
Magistrates' and Crow Payers' Declarations,	1876-77	—	1
Presentment Books,	1877	30	—
Presentments,	"	—	3
Publicans' License Notices,	1876-7	—	1
" " Register,	"	1	—
Renewal Affidavits,	1877	—	1
Returns and Orders,	"	—	1
Tolls and Customs Schedules,	1818-59	—	1
Voters' Registers and Lists,	1877	—	1
Witnesses' Expenses Book (Trials),	1851-77	1	—

53. From the Crown and Peace Office of the county of Kildare :—

Records.	Date.	Vols.	Pris.
Civil Bill Papers,	1877	—	1
Convictions, Records of,	1875-7	—	1
Coroners' Inquests,	1877	—	1
Crown Files at Assizes,	"	—	1
" " Quarter Sessions,	"	—	1
Jurors' Book,	"	1	—
" Lists,	"	—	1
Landlord and Tenant (1870) Act : Papers,	"	—	1
Maps, Plans, Awards, &c.,	"	—	1
Presentments,	"	—	3
Probate Paper,	"	—	1
Publicans' License Notices,	1876-7	—	1
Query Books,	1877	2	..
Renewal Affidavits,	"	—	1
Trees, Affidavit to register,	"	—	1
Voters' Registers and Lists,	1876-7	—	1

54. From the Crown and Peace Office of the King's county :—

Records.	Date.	Vols.	Pcds.
Civil Bill Books, ...	1876-77	4	—
„ „ Papers, ...	1877	—	1
Coroners' Inquests, ...	1876-77	—	1
Crown Files at Assizes, ...	1877	—	1
„ „ „ Quarter Sessions, ...	„	—	1
Jurors' Lists, ...	„	—	1
Landlord and Tenant (1870) Act: Papers, . . .	„	—	1
Magistrates' and Cess Payers' Declarations, . .	„	—	1
Maps, Plans, Awards, &c., ...	„	—	1
Presentment Books, ...	„	1	—
Presentments, ...	„	—	1
Publicans' Licence Lists, &c., ...	„	—	1
Removal Affidavits, ...	„	—	1
Trees, Affidavit to register, ...	„	—	1
Voters' Registers, Lists, &c., ...	„	—	1

55. From the Crown and Peace Office of the county of Limerick :—

Records.	Date.	Vols.	Pcds.
Appeals to Assizes, ...	1877	—	1
Civil Bill Book, ...	1876-7	2	—
„ „ and Ejectment Books (Chairman's), .	„	2	—
„ „ Papers, ...	1877	—	1
Coroners' Inquests, ...	„	—	1
Crown Book at Assizes, ...	„	1	—
„ „ „ Quarter Sessions (Chairman's), . .	1876-7	1	—
„ „ Files at Assizes, ...	1877	—	1
„ „ „ Quarter Sessions, ...	„	—	1
Fishery Papers, ...	„	—	1
Freemasons' and Friendly Brothers' Memorials, .	„	—	1
Jurors' Affidavits to remit Fines, ...	„	—	1
„ Books, ...	„	1	—
„ Lists, ...	„	—	1
Landlord and Tenant (1870) Act: Papers, . .	„	—	1
Maps, Plans, Awards, &c., ...	„	—	1
Presentment Books (City), ...	„	1	—
Probate Papers, ...	„	—	1
Protection Order (Married Women), . . .	„	—	1

CROWN AND PEACE OFFICE, COUNTY OF LIMERICK—*continued*.

Records.	Date.	Vols.	Parts.
Publicans' Licence Notices, ...	1876-7	—	1
" " Register (Renewal Certificates), . . .	"	1	—
Quarry Books, ...	1877	2	—
Renewal Affidavits, ...	"	—	1
Returns and Orders (Government), ...	1876-8	—	1
Town Commissioners' (Rathkeale) Accounts, ...	"	—	1
Voters' Lists, ...	1877	—	1

56. From the Crown and Peace Office of the county and city of Londonderry:—

Records.	Date.	Vols.	Parts.
Appeals to Assizes, ...	1877	—	1
Civil Bill Books, ...	1873-77	2	—
" Papers, ...	1877	—	1
Coroners' Inquests, ...	1876-77	—	2
Crown Book at Assizes (Court Book), ...	1877	1	—
" Fiats	"	—	1
" " Quarter Sessions, ...	"	—	1
Jurors' Book, ...	"	1	—
" Lists, ...	"	—	1
Landlord and Tenant (1870) Act : Papers, ...	"	—	1
Magistrates' and Clerk Payers' Declarations, . . .	"	—	1
Presentment Books, ...	"	16	—
Presentments, ...	"	—	2
Process Servers' Books, ...	1874-7	3	—
Voters' Registers and Lists, ...	1877	—	1

57. From the Crown and Peace Office of the county of Longford:—

Records.	Date.	Vols.	Parts.
Civil Bill Books, ...	1871-77	4	—
" " Papers, ...	1877	—	1
Coroners' Inquests, ...	"	—	1
Crown Files at Assizes, ...	"	—	1
" " " Quarter Sessions, ...	"	—	1
Ejectment Books, ...	1872-77	2	—
Presentment Books, ...	1877	2	—
Quarry Books, ...	"	2	—

58. From the Crown and Peace Office of the county of Louth :—

Records.	Date.	Vols.	Pres.
Appeals to Assizes, ...	1876-7	—	1
Civil Bill Book (Dundalk), ...	1868-77	1	—
„ „ Papers, ...	1877	—	1
Convictions (Summary), ...	1876-7	—	1
Coroners' Inquests, ...	1876-7	—	1
Crown Files at Assizes, ...	1877	—	1
„ „ „ Quarter Sessions, ...	„	—	1
Fishery Papers, ...	1876-7	—	1
Freemasons' Memorials, ...	„	—	1
Jurors' Books, ...	1877	1	—
„ Lists, ...	„	—	1
Presentment Books (Abstracts), ...	1876-7	2	—
„ (undischarged) Book, ...	1876-77	1	—
Presentments, ...	1877	—	1
Proclamations, ...	„	—	1
Query Books, ...	1876-7	8	—
Sessions (Petty) Papers (Alteration of Dates), .	1876-6	—	1
Voters' Registers, Lists, Claims, and Objections,	1876-7	—	1

59. From the Crown and Peace Office of the county of Mayo :—

Records.	Date.	Vols.	Pres.
Attorneys, List of, ...	1876-7	—	1
Civil Bill Books, ...	1871-7	6	1
„ „ Papers, ...	1877	—	1
Coroners' Inquests, ...	1876-7	—	1
Crown Books at Assizes, ...	1877	8	—
„ Book at Quarter Sessions, ...	„	1	—
„ Files at Assizes, ...	„	—	1
„ „ „ Quarter Sessions, ...	„	—	1
Fishery Papers, ...	„	—	1
Freemasons' Memorial, ...	„	—	1
Informations, Receipt Book for, ...	1876-7	1	—
Jurors' Books, ...	1876-7	4	—
„ Lists, ...	1877	—	1
Landlord and Tenant Act (1870) : Papers,. .	„	—	1
Maps, Plans, &c., ...	„	—	1

CROWN AND PEACE OFFICE, COUNTY OF MAYO—continued.

Records.	Date.	Vol.	Prch.
Militia Returns	1877	—	1
Presentment Books, ...	„	23	—
„ Papers, ...	„	—	1
Presentments, Schedules of, ...	„	2	—
Probate Papers, ...	1873-7	—	1
Proces Servers' Books	1877	32	—
Publicans' License Certificate Books, . . .	1876-7	2	—
„ „ Lists and Notices, .	1876-7	—	1
Quarry Books	1877	1	—
Renewal Affidavits, ...	1871-7	—	3
Returns, Orders, and Correspondence, . .	1877	—	1
Voters' Lists, Claims, &c., ...	„	—	1

60. From the Crown and Peace Office of the county of Meath :—

Records.	Date.	Vol.	Prch.
Civil Bill Papers, ...	1877	—	1
Coroners' Inquests, ...	1874-5	—	1
Crown Files at Assizes, ...	1877	—	1
„ „ „ Quarter Sessions, ...	„	—	1
Voters' Lists, ...	1876-7	8	—

61. From the Crown and Peace Office of the county of Monaghan :—

Records.	Date.	Vols.	Prch.
Appeals to Assizes, ...	1877	—	1
„ „ Quarter Sessions, ...	1876-7	—	1
Attorneys, List of, ...	1873	—	1
Civil Bill Papers, ...	1877	—	1
Convictions (Summary), ...	1876-77	—	1
Coroners' Inquests, ...	1877	—	1
Crown Files at Assizes, ...	„	—	1
„ „ „ Quarter Sessions, ...	„	—	1
Ejectment Books (Duplicates), ...	„	—	1
Estreat Order Book, ...	1833-6	1	—

CROWN AND PEACE OFFICE, COUNTY OF MONAGHAN—*continued.*

Records.	Date.	Vols.	Pkts.
Fishery Papers, ...	1876	—	1
Jurors' Lists, ...	1876-7	—	1
Landlord and Tenant (1870) Act : Papers, .	1877	—	1
Legacy Book, ...	"	1	—
Magistrates' and Cess Payers' Declarations, .	"	—	1
Maps, Plans, Awards, &c., ...	"	—	1
Presentment Books, ...	"	11	—
Presentments, ...	"	—	1
Probate Papers, ...	"	—	1
Process Server's Book, ...	1876-7	1	—
Query Book, ...	1877	1	—
Renewal Affidavits, ...	"	—	1
Returns and Correspondence, ...	1876-7	—	1
Sessions (Petty) Clerks' Appointments, . .	1877	—	1
Spirit Licence Notices, ...	1876-7	—	1
Statutes, ...	1875-6	—	1
Trees, Affidavit to register, ...	1877	—	1
Voters' Notices of Claims and Objections, .	"	—	1
.. Registers and Lists (bound), . . .	1876-7	6	—
.. .. .. (unbound), . . .	1877	—	1
.. Registration Papers, ...	"	—	1

62. From the Crown and Peace Office of the Queen's county:—

Records.	Date.	Vols.	Pkts.
Civil Bill Papers, ...	1877	—	1
Coroners' Inquests, ...	"	—	1
Crown Files at Assizes, ...	"	—	1
.. .. .. Quarter Sessions, . . .	"	—	1
Jurors' Lists, ...	"	—	1
Landlord and Tenant (1870) Act : Papers, .	"	—	1
Magistrates' and Cess Payers' Declarations, .	"	—	1
Maps, Plans, Awards, &c., ...	"	—	1
Presentments, ...	"	—	1
Proclamations, ...	"	—	1
Publicans' Licence Notices, ...	1876-7	—	1
Query Books, ...	1877	2	—
Renewal Affidavits, ...	"	—	1
Voters' Registers, Lists, Claims, and Objections, .	"	—	1

63. From the Crown and Peace Office of the county of Roscommon :—

Records.	Date.	Vols.	Prels.
Appeals to Assizes	1877	—	1
Ejectment Book, ...	1862–77	1	—
Jurors' Book, ...	1877	1	—
„ Lists, ...	1878	—	1
Landlord and Tenant (1870) Act : Book, ...	1870–73	1	—
„ „ „ „ Papers, ...	1851–77	3	—
Process Servers' Books, ...	1864–77	8	—
Publicans' Licence Register, ...	1874–76	1	—
Quarry Book , ...	1874	1	—
Town Commissioners' Accounts, ...	1876–77	—	1
Trees, Affidavit to Register, ...	1876	—	1
Voters' Registers, Lists, Claims, &c.	„	—	1

64. From the Crown and Peace Office of the county of Sligo :—

Records.	Date.	Vols.	Prels.
Appeals to Assizes, ...	1877	—	1
Civil Bill Books, ...	„	3	—
Coroners' Inquests, ...	—	—	1
Crown Book at Assizes, ...	1876–77	1	—
„ Files „	1877	—	1
„ „ „ Quarter Sessions, ...	„	—	1
Jurors' Books, ...	„	3	—
Presentments, ...	„	—	1
Presentment Books, ...	„	13	—
„ (Abstract) Book, ...	„	1	—
Publicans' Licence Notices, ...	„	—	1
Quarry Book, ...	„	1	—
Renewal Affidavits, ...	„	—	1
Voters' Register and Lists, ...	„	—	1

65. From the Crown and Peace Office of the county of Tipperary :—

Records	Date.	Vols.	Pcls.
Civil Bill Books, ...	1877	5	—
„ „ Papers (Miscellaneous), ...	„	—	1
Clerk of the Peace, Affidavit of, ...	„	—	1
County Court Judge's Declaration, ...	„	—	1
Crown Files at Assizes, ...	„	—	1
„ „ „ Quarter Sessions, ...	„	—	1
Ejectment Processes, ...	„	—	1
Jurors' Books, ...	„	1	—
„ Petitions against Fines, ...	1874-7	—	1
Levy Fund Rule, ...	1877	—	1
Presentments, ...	„	—	1
Probate Papers, ...	1875-7	—	1
Publicans' Registers, ...	187-	—	1
Renewal Affidavits, ...	1877	—	1
Voters' Lists, ...	„	—	1
„ Registers, ...	„	1	—

66. From the Crown and Peace Office of the county of Westmeath :—

Records.	Date.	Vols.	Pcls.
Appeals to Assizes, ...	1877	—	1
Civil Bill Book, ...	1866-77	1	—
„ „ Papers, ...	1877	—	1
Coroners' Inquests, ...	1876-77	—	1
Crown Book at Assizes (Judges'), ...	1877	1	—
„ Files „ „ „	„	—	1
„ Book at Quarter Sessions (Music), . . .	1866-77	1	—
„ Files „ „	1877	—	1
Jurors' Books, ...	„	1	—
Maps, Plans, Awards, &c., ...	„	—	1
Presentment Books, ...	„	2	—
Presentments, ...	„	—	2
Publicans' License Notices, ...	„	—	1
Query Books, ...	„	1	—

67. From the Crown and Peace Office of the county of Wexford :—

Records.	Date.	Vols.	Prcls.
Accounts (Town Commissioners, &c.),	1876-8	—	1
Appeals to Assizes,	1877	—	1
Coroners' Inquests,	1876-7	—	1
Crown Book at Assizes,	1877	1	—
„ Books at Quarter Sessions,	1876-7	7	—
Files at Assizes,	1877	—	1
„ „ „ Quarter Sessions,	„	—	1
Election Processes,	„	—	1
Freemasons' Registration Memorials,	1871-7	—	1
Jurors' Books,	1877	2	—
„ Lists,	„	—	1
Magistrates' Attendance at Petty Sessions, Returns of,	„	—	1
„ Letters of Appointment, &c.,	1876-7	—	1
„ Lists,	1872-6	—	1
Maps, Plans, Awards, &c.,	1878	—	1
Presentment Books,	1877	23	—
Presentments,	—	—	8
Probate Papers,	1871-7	—	1
Publicans' Licence Notices,	1876-7	—	1
Query Books,	1877	3	—
Records of Convictions,	1876-7	—	1
Renewal Affidavits,	1877	—	8
Returns of Criminals,	1849-77	—	1
Returns, Orders, and Correspondence,	1876-7	—	1
Sessions (Petty) Districts Alteration, &c. Papers,	1866-77	—	3
Statutes and Gazettes,	1870-7	—	1
Wexford Harbour Bye Laws,	1878	—	1
Wild Fowl Preservation (1876) Act : Papers,	1877	—	1

68. From the Crown and Peace Office of the county of Wicklow :—

Records.	Date.	Vols.	Prcls.
Appeals to Assizes,	1876-7	—	1
Civil Bill Book (Chairman's),	1877	1	—
„ „ Papers,	„	—	1
Coroners' Inquests,	„	—	1

CROWN AND PEACE OFFICE, COUNTY OF WICKLOW—*continued*.

Records.	Date.	Vols.	Pcls.
Crown Book at Assizes, ...	1877	1	—
„ Files	„	—	1
„ „ „ Quarter Sessions, ...	„	—	1
Pickery Papers, ...	1876-7	—	1
Jurors' Lists, ...	1877	—	1
Landlord and Tenant (1870) Act: Papers, . . .	„	—	1
Maps, Plans, Awards, &c., ...	„	—	1
Presentment Books, ...	1870-7	13	—
„ „ (Abstracts), ...	1850-0	—	1
„ „ (Schedules of Application), . . .	1877	2	—
„ „ (Payment) Books, ...	1868-77	10	—
Presentments, ...	1877	—	1
Treasurers' Bank Books, ...	1844-71	10	—
Valuation Books, ...	1844 and 1850-77	20	—
Voters' Registers and Lists, ...	1877	—	1

69. From J. H. Samuels, Esq., Registrar of the Diocese of Dublin :—

Records.	Date.	Vols.	Pcls.
Dublin Diocese Caveat Book, ...	1838-41		
„ „ Marriage License Book, . . .	1838-47	3	—
„ „ Register, ...	1838-47		

70. From Mr. J. Coleman, Limerick (Purchased) :—

Records.	Date.	Vols.	Pcls.
Diocesan Records of Killaloe and Kilfenora :—			
Bond, Marriage License, ...	1740	—	1
Bonds, Administration, ...	1729-55	—	1
Cause Papers, ...	1608-1840	—	8
Consistorial Court Act Books, ...	1713-94	5	1
Copy Deed : Viscount Ross to Arthur Parsons and others,	1682	—	1
Procuration Rolls (Visitations), ...	1800-18	—	3
Visitation Books (Kilfenora), ...	1749-1840	2	—
„ „ Notice of, ...	1788	—	1

71. From Sir Thomas Phillipps' Library (Purchased):—

Records.	Date.	Vols.	Prod.
Assessment and Appointment Book, Parish of K. kenane,	1853	1	—
" " " " Dathpatrick,	1854	1	—
Entry Book of Letters (Commissioners of the Revenue, for granting possession of forfeited lands),	1691-2	1	—

72. On 21st July, 1898, Rev. Christopher T. M'Cready, D.D.
presented to this department the ancient Vestry Book of the
parish of St. Andrew, Dublin, which had become his property;
the volume extends from 16th April, 1636, to 8th November,
1702.

73. Deeds affecting the right of the Crown were deposited
here by the Quit Rent Office during the year, to the number
of ninety-three, of which eighty-four are conveyances of
Crown and Quit Rents.

Sorting and Arrangement of Records.

74. The re-arrangement of the Equity Exchequer Bills has pro-
gressed from October, 1764, to January, 1788, and of the
Answers from January, 1764, to November, 1737, comprising
5,435 fascicoli, assorted into 916 brown paper parcels.

75. One thousand seven hundred and eighteen bundles of
Crown and Peace Office Records, 184 bundles of the late Landed
Estates Court Records, and 517 bundles of the Census Returns
for 1841 have been cleaned, stamped and parcelled into brown
paper dust-proof parcels.

76. One thousand nine hundred and fifty-eight Bankruptcy
files in portfolios have been cleaned, newly corded, stamped,
and labelled.

77. One hundred and forty-eight bundles of Building Papers,
Glebe Title Deeds, Maps and Terriers, and See Leases of various
dioceses, have been folded to an uniform size and arranged in
covered parcels; as have also 316 bundles of Exchequer Plead-
ings and Papers.

78. The arrangement and consolidation of the Cause Papers of
the Court of Chancery, commonly called Masters' Papers, have
advanced as far as the end of letter N, making 11,277 bundles of
Cause Papers.

79. Three thousand one hundred and seventy-six Marriage
Licence Bonds of the Diocese of Cloyne have been repaired,
sized, and pasted on guards, and twelve volumes of them bound.
Two hundred and fifteen leaves of Parish Registers have been
repaired and sized, and 124 volumes of Records, 277 volumes of
specifications and patents of invention, and eleven volumes of
indexes, have been bound.

Indexing and Calendaring.

80. An Index has been made to a Will and Grant Book of the Diocese of Ferns for the years 1791-1800, to a like volume of the Diocese of Leighlin for the years 1666-1801, to a Grant Book of the Diocese of Ardfert for the years 1780-1788, to a Cork and Cloyne Marriage Licence Book for the years 1776-1780, and to a Diocesan Registry and Will and Grant Book (Diocese of Clonfert), 1710-1754.

81. An Index has been made to the Decretal Orders on Cause Petitions under the Chancery (Ireland) Regulation Act, 1850, and to the series of Masters' Orders in Chancery for the years 1850-55.

82. The Marriage Licence Bonds of the Diocese of Ossory have been indexed, and the engrossment has been bound for the use of the public.

83. The Indices to the Wills of the Dioceses of Ireland, with the exception of Dublin (which has been already printed), are in process of being compared with the original Wills and checked with the Will Books, and it is expected that the long-deferred work of preparing for press a general Consolidated Index of these Wills can soon be undertaken.

Proceedings under the Parochial Records Acts, 38 & 39 Vict., c. 59, and 39 & 40 Vict., c. 58.

84. The Report of Parochial Officers having custody of their Parish Registers under Retention Orders were all duly furnished.

85. The Retention Orders granted by the Master of the Rolls up to the commencement of the present year are 881 in number.

86. Registers of the following Parishes were repaired and bound at the request of the respective custodians, viz.:—Bally-adams, 1 vol., Cloyne, 4 vols., St. Peter's, Dublin, 2 vols., Stradbally (Leighlin), 2 vols.

87. The Records of the following parishes, which became attachable during the year 1898, have been transferred to this Department:—

Parish.	County.	Vols.	Baptisms.	Marriages.	Burials.
Glenties, ...	Donegal, .	2	1842-1887	—	1842-1887
Kilrossa, ...	Waterford, .	2	1849-1853	—	1849-1861
Kiltyclogher, . . .	Leitrim, .	1	1828-1878	—	1828-1878
Newtownards, . . .	Down, . . .	11	1713-1728 / 1837-1884	1701-1723 / 1805 / 1832-1845	1701-1728 / 1833-1885
St. John's, Kilkenny, . .	Kilkenny, .	3	1848-1900	1849-1884	1848-1884

88. In the following parishes the Records were allowed to remain in local custody under Retention Orders:—

Aghalee. | St. John's, Monkstown.
Ballis. | Stratford-on-Slaney.
Cappagh. | Toureen.
Newtownbarry. |

89. The Master of the Rolls cancelled the Retention Order for the parish of Magheragall, and issued a new one on 26th July, 1898, in consequence of the erection of a vestry room, which necessitated the removal and re-erection of the safe.

90. The Retention Order, which had been granted for the parish of Eirke in 1879, was cancelled by Order of the Master of the Rolls, dated 11th May, 1898, and under the same order two Registers were transferred to this Office. This step was taken in consequence of the loss of a vestry book, containing entries of Baptisms, 1762-0, which had been included in the Retention Order.

91. A Register of the parishes of Templeton and Nohoval, 1745-1784, which was not returned in the original inventory, was recovered by Rev. Geo. Herrick, Incumbent, and deposited here under warrant of the Master of the Rolls.

92. The fees received in stamps during the year reached the total of £983 3s. 6d., an amount which shows an increase of £122 6s. on the receipts of the previous year.

TABLE OF FEES, 1898.

Month.	Inspections.	Traces of Maps.	Attendances.	Folios at 1s.	Folios at 6d.	Amount.
						£ s. d.
January,	193	1	—	453	2,518	95 0 0
February,	253	3	—	342	2,152	88 13 6
March,	315	3	—	501	2,539	105 9 0
April,	177	7	—	607	2,857	82 9 0
May,	258	1	—	183	1,501	61 2 6
June,	309	5	1	681	2,396	115 16 0
July,	261	4	—	356	1,804	78 11 6
August,	194	3	—	69	1,113	41 9 8
September,	151	1	—	133	1,800	84 5 0
October,	292	8	—	122	2,135	73 8 0
November,	272	1	—	151	2,708	85 0 0
December,	303	4	—	89	2,471	79 9 8
Total	2,854	39	1	3,708	38,537	955 5 4

In addition to the above, fees on copies made for Public Departments have been remitted to the amount of £50 8s. 6d.

93. I have to acknowledge the following donations:—

Two copies of "An Index to the Prerogative Wills of Ireland, 1536-1810," by the editor, Sir Arthur Vicars, F.S.A., Ulster King of Arms.

"A Bibliography of Works of William Reeves, D.D., late Lord Bishop of Down, Connor, and Dromore," by the author, J. R. Garstin, D.D., F.S.A.

"A Short History of the Royal Longford Militia, 1793-1893," by H. A. Richey, esq., B.L., the author.

"Register of Wills and Inventories, Diocese of Dublin, 1457-1483; edited by H. F. Berry, esq., M.A.," by the Royal Society of Antiquaries of Ireland.

"Walker's Hibernian Magazine," 1774–5, 1784, 1791.
Parts 1 and 2, by the Rev. W. A. Reynell, B.D.

"History of the Earlier Years of the Funded Debt, 1694–1786," by the Comptroller-General, National Debt Office.

"Studies on the Red Book of the Exchequer," by the author, J. H. Round, esq., M.A.

"Index to Marriage Licence Bonds, Diocese of Cork and Ross, 1623–1750, edited by Mr. H. W. Gillman," by the Cork Archæological Society.

94. A large number of Searches dealing with matters of historical and antiquarian interest have been made during the year. Among these I may mention more particularly the History of the Counties of Clare, Fermanagh, and Monaghan; of the Parishes of Ardee, Clonfert, Derrybrush, Errigal Trough, Killucan, Monkstown, Tallaght, and Tullylish; of Carrickfergus, Waterford, Thomascourt, Mount Merrion, Limerick Cathedral, Dublin Hospitals, and Dublin Printing in the 17th Century; of the O'Carrolls of Ely, and the families of County Fermanagh; of the 68th Regiment; the Cromwellian Settlement of Ireland; the Military and Civil History of the year 1798; the life of William Molyneux, of Dublin, and materials for contributions to the Dictionary of National Biography.

Dated at the Public Record Office,
Four Courts, Dublin, this Fifth
day of May, 1899.

J. J. DIGGES LA TOUCHE,

Deputy Keeper of the Public Records and Keeper of the State Papers in Ireland.

I humbly certify to your Excellency that this Report is made by the Deputy Keeper of the Public Records and Keeper of the State Papers in Ireland, under my direction, pursuant to the Statute.

A. M. PORTER,

Master of the Rolls.

APPENDIX J.

Corrections to the Addenda to the Dublin Grants Index, 1272–1800.
(Appendix III., 26th Report.)

At the time of making the Addenda to the above Index, the original Marriage Licence Books for the periods 1672–1687, 1712–1741, were supposed to be lost, and the Addenda was compiled from a MS. Index in the possession of H. Farnham Burke, Esq., Somerset Herald. The original books were, however, found in 1897 among the Rule Books in the Registrar's Office of the Diocese of Dublin, and were removed here; they are as follows:—

Reference to Volume.	Subject.	Date.
1 L : 13 : D.	Marriage Licence Book, ...	7 Nov., 1672–3 Aug., 1684
1 L : 13 : 31.	"Book of Entryes for Lycences both in the Consistory and Archdeacon's Regr. of the Diocese of Dublin."	7 Mar., 1712–17 Oct., 1732
1 L : 13 : 39,	"Entries of Marriage Lycences beginning the 17 day of October, 1721."	17 Oct., 1721–23 Oct., 1728
1 L : 13 : 40.	"Entries of Marriage Licences beginning the 23 October, 1728."	23 Oct., 1728–24 Oct., 1741.

They have been indexed, and the following entries in the original books were found to have been incorrectly given or omitted in the copies used for the Addenda :—

CORRECTIONS, DUBLIN GRANT INDEX, 1272–1800.

Name, Place, and Occupation.	Year.	Nature of Record.	Page.
Abbott, Elizabeth and Benjamin Husband, . . .	1739	M.L.	163
Abidie, Abigail and John Jackson, ...	1673	M.L.	3
Adair, Archibald and Frances Crozier, widow, . .	1733	M.L.	6
Adams, Mary and John Wellman, ...	1726	M.L.	191
„ Sarah and James Lane, ...	1728	M.L.	13
Adcock, Richard and Mildred Johnston. . . .	1737	M.L.	173
Addy, Richard and Judith Shippabottom. . . .	1729	M.L.	204
Adkinson, Margaret (widow) and William Alencie, . .	1673	M.L.	33
Aghmaty, Thomas and Anne Mary King. . . .	1733	M.L.	11
Agitt, Joseph and Frances Hardiff. . . .	1740	M.L.	63
Agun, Margaret and Thomas Iredall, . . .	1711	M.I.	16
Alakin, James and Lucy Barrel, ...	1684	M.L.	78
„ James and Susannah Johnston, . .	1729	M.L.	203
„ Ruth (widow) and John White, . .	1733	M.L.	6

CORRECTIONS, DUBLIN GRANT INDEX, 1272-1800—*continued.*

Name, Place, and Occupation.	Year.	Nature of Record.	Page.
Aiguis, Francis and Samuel Morton, . . .	1729	M.L.	65
Aish, Elizabeth and William Greenway, . .	1729	M.L.	67
Albrittain, Elizabeth (widow) and Thomas Moore, . .	1727	M.L.	63
Albritton, Thomas and Elizabeth Cole, . . .	1759	B.L.	71
Almack, Anna Maria and Robert Snow, . . .	1710	M.L.	67
Aldas, Charles and Eliza Murphy, . . .	1740	M.L.	165
Ales, Mary and Joseph Howell, . . .	1662	M.L.	9
Alexander, Jane and William Williams, . . .	1730	M.L.	9
Alexander, Anne (widow) and Cornelius Tegart, . .	1797	M.L.	6
Allison, Elizabeth and Ralph Campbell, . .	1729	M.L.	60
Alkin, Martha and Rev. Bedingham Swan, . .	1729	M.L.	65
" Robert and Rebecca Cooley, . . .	1672	M.L.	1
" Thomas and Barbara Smith, widow, . .	1679	M.L.	63
Allcock, Joseph and Glen Harper, widow, . .	1729	M.L.	64
Allen, Bridget and Peter Cawthren, . .	1729	M.L.	160
" Frances and Thomas Pitts, . .	1753	M.L.	121
" Jane (widow) and Patrick Cannon, . .	1735	M.L.	63
" John and Anne Smith, . .	1739	M.L.	9
" John and Frances Walsh, . . .	1729	M.L.	160
Allvanen, Joseph and Sarah Dawson, . . .	1731	M.L.	159
Allisson, John and Mary Styng, . . .	1727	M.L.	114
" Joseph and Margaret Lynch, widow, . .	1726	M.L.	128
Allmarry, Margaret (widow) and John Oatherwood, .	1728	M.L.	126
Allan, Sarah (widow) and Adrian Buckley, . .	1725	M.L.	29
Ally, George and Biddy Aston, . . .	1729	M.L.	67
Almega, Carothers (widow) and John Hudson, . .	1661	M.L.	73
Ambery, Elizabeth and William Ivthin, . .	1663	M.L.	39
Ambery, Jane and Joseph Lewis, . . .	737	M.I.	170
Anderson, Thomas and Elizabeth Standering, . .	1783	M.L.	135
Anderton, Thomas and Elizabeth Berry, . .	1663	M.L.	71
Ando, Mary and Walter Fotterall, . . .	1734	M.L.	63
Andrews, Richard and Margaret Broff, widow, . .	1701	M.L.	113
" Ursula (widow) and Christopher Meaines, .	1671	M.L.	63
Annesley, William and Sarah Jones, . . .	1729	M.L.	67
Ansdall, Samuel and Elizabeth Sinclare, . .	1711	M.L.	130
Appleberry, William and Jane Chapman, widow, .	1679	M.L.	64
Arbuckle, James and Mary Ham, widow, . .	1729	M.L.	64
Archbald, Simon and Elinor Cussak, . . .	1671	M.L.	6
Archer, Elizabeth and John Swords, . . .	1711	M.L.	60

CORRECTIONS, DUBLIN GRANT INDEX, 1272-1800—*continued.*

Name, Place, and Occupation.	Year.	Nature of Record.	Page.
Ardesia, Malburis and Mary Holland.	1780	M.L.	98
Arkinson, Martha and John Davies,	1785	M.L.	69
Armengaud, Louisa (widow) and John Desandres,	1733	M.L.	17
Armstronge, Anne and Henry Shirrow,	1673	M.L.	6
Argstead, Dorothy and Richard Sassl,	1781	M.L.	165
Armstrong, Mary (widow) and William Meredith,	1749	M.L.	10
Ashbourner, Elizabeth and Bernard Demess,	1731	M.L.	13
Ashburner, Sarah and Aaron Edwards,	1727	M.L.	44
Ashby, John and Elizabeth Nelson,	1780	M.L.	85
Ashmehurst, Anne and John Lease,	1671	M.L.	4
Ashley, Winifred and Stephen Nix,	1718	M.L.	23
Ashmoure, Rebecca and John Davies,	1735	M.L.	101
Ashton, Elizabeth and Gilbert Barlow,	1729	M.L.	68
„ Joseph and Elinor Locke,	1711	M.L.	38
Aston, Elizabeth and Monson Bell,	1733	M.L.	31
„ Elizabeth (widow) and John Donalan,	1675	M.L.	14
„ Jane and Charles Feilden,	1671	M.L.	19
„ Hely and George Ally,	1739	M.L.	47
„ Thomas (Rev.) and Mary Smith,	1673	M.L.	31
Aston, Mary and William Fuller,	1679	M.L.	7
Auamruthy, Jane and Charles Healty,	1749	M.L.	75
Auchmuty, Helen and Tobias Dodd,	1722	M.L.	6
Babbington, Catherine (widow) and John Piggot,	1729	M.L.	63
Bahn, Charlotte and Charles Newcomen,	1749	M.L.	99
Badumh, Joseph and Anne Question,	1714	M.L.	10
Baggee, Boyle and Hannah Bownest,	1728	M.L.	23
Bagge, Isham and Mary Francis,	1717	M.L.	40
Bagly, Edward and Anne Hoche,	1677	M.L.	91
Bagnall, Mary and Thomas Warren,	1659	M.L.	71
Bagot, Charles and Temperance Brown,	1739	M.L.	81
Baker, Elizabeth and Abraham Tobin,	1731	M.L.	161
„ Elinor (widow) and John Clark,	1741	M.L.	100
„ James and Anne Graham,	1684	M.L.	78
Baldwin, John and Mary Wall,	1734	M.L.	66
Ball, Anne and Steven Williamson,	1685	M.L.	43
„ Mary and Thomas Perrit,	1711	M.L.	13
„ Nichols and Catherine Pryan,	1733	M.L.	24

CORRECTIONS, DUBLIN GRANT INDEX, 1272–1800—continued.

Name, Place, and Occupation.	Year.	Nature of Record.	Page.
Ballance, James and Margaret Kenney,	1787	M.L.	141
Ballard, William and Margaret Hyde, .	1726	M.L.	141
Ballidin, Elizabeth (widow) and John Williams,	1757	M.L.	114
Ballentine, Hannah and Hugh Picknoll,	1735	M.L.	73
Bambricks, Joan and Gilbert Wall,	1678	M.L.	11
Bambrack, Elizabeth and Richard Pindar,	1731	M.L.	113
Banford, Catherine and William Krarm,	1740	M.L.	73
Banks, Eleanor (widow) and Thomas Barrit,	1671	M.L.	1
„ Thomas and Mary Feilding, widow,	1733	M.L.	13
Baroifre, Antboinette and Peter Cousins Balosel,	1735	M.L.	71
Barker, Alice and John Brewster,	1681	M.L.	12
„ Allen and Elizabeth Ellison,	1676	M.L.	3
„ Charles and Mary Nogent,	1741	M.L.	111
„ John and Elizabeth Leviv,	1653	M.L.	6
„ John and Comfort Bane,	1789	M.L.	141,118
Barlow, Gilbert and Elizabeth Ashton,	1729	M.L.	11
Barnes, Humphry and Jane Mounslow, widow,	1713	M.L.	1
Baralston, Elizabeth and James Fiszmaurice,	1693	M.L.	8
Barret, Belinda and James Hackett,	1726	M.L.	118
„ Jane and John Conely,	1733	M.L.	13
„ Lucy and James Aickin,	1684	M.L.	3
Barrett, Ruth (widow) and Matthew Cape,	1787	M.L.	123
Barry, Elizabeth and Thomas Anderton,	1685	M.L.	71
Barton, Anne and Charles Fellows,	1790	M.L.	8
Bassa, Elizabeth (widow) and John Govers,	1726	M.L.	113
Bathoe, Margaret and John Gormley,	1678	M.L.	3
Battersby, William (junior) and Mary Garnett,	1788	M.L.	139
Beamford, Grace and Samuel Gordon,	1777	M.L.	11
Bayly, Walter Chapland and Elizabeth Way,	1728	M.L.	6
Beatagh, Margaret (widow) and John Withom,	1678	M.L.	3
Beatly, Edward and Mary Brock,	1740	M.L.	6
Beatter, Robert and Catherine Cougrave,	1686	M.L.	3
Beaver, Martha and Latham Blackey,	1733	M.L.	1
Beckett, Anna (widow) and Joseph Kathern,	1674	M.L.	1
Beddy, John and Rebecca Faulkner,	1729	M.L.	4
Beeby, Nathaniel and Hannah Bewley, .	1728	M.L.	127
Begral, Francis and Jane Gantier,	1689	M.L.	73
Bell, Mossum and Elizabeth Aston,	1722	M.L.	9
„ Thomas and Alice Stephens,	1684	M.L.	71

Corrections, Dublin Grant Index, 1272–1800—continued.

Name, Place, and Occupation.	Year.	Nature of Record.	Page.
Bellers, Charles and Mary Woods, ...	1773	M.L.	48
Bellwood, Henry and Jane Bulkeley, widow, . .	1719	M.L.	3
„ Henry and Frances Pearson, widow, . .	1733	M.L.	131
Bennett, Christopher and Anne Westmorland, widow. .	1677	M.L.	29
„ Eleanor and Joseph Withington. . .	1693	M.L.	67
„ Thomas and Alice Houghton, . . .	1841	M.L.	590
Benson, Barnard and Elizabeth Ashbourne, . .	1724	M.L.	62
„ Emy and Hugh Massey, ...	1691	M.L.	50
Berry, Mary and Isaac Heatly, ...	1731	M.L.	115
Barlow, Jeremiah and Susan Whitmore, widow, .	1690	M.L.	69
Bertrand, John and Sarah Elizabeth Cartwright, .	1737	M.L.	166
Bery, Jane and Yemeny St. Vast, . . .	1673	M.L.	27
Betagh, William and Mary Obryan, . . .	1723	M.L.	3
Bewley, Hannah and Nathaniel Derby, . .	1731	M.L.	127
Bibby, Elizabeth and Joy Whitmore, . .	1741	M.L.	123
Bignall, Hugh and Elizabeth Cornwell, . .	1693	M.L.	78
„ Mary and William New, . . .	1711	M.L.	16
Bill, Martha and William Tomlin, . .	1691	M.L.	61
Billingsly, Anne (widow) and John Lovett, . .	1699	M.L.	45
„ William and Mary Fleming, widow, .	1715	M.L.	6
Bingham, Elizabeth and John Casey, . .	1671	M.L.	9
Birch, Elinor and James Boulton, . .	1723	M.L.	123
Bird, Dolphina and John Tallon, . .	1711	M.L.	129
„ Thomas and Jane Liford, . .	1671	M.L.	8
Birkett, Mary and Henry Evans, . .	1699	M.L.	67
Blackford, Catherine (widow) and Thomas Moore, .	1738	M.L.	103
Blacker, Lathum and Martha Beaver, . .	1726	M.L.	6
Blackmore, Mary and Joseph Gayer, . .	1694	M.L.	79
Blacknay, Elizabeth and Henry Road, . .	1685	M.L.	60
Blake, Elizabeth (widow) and William Devenish, .	1729	M.L.	64
„ Sibella and William Lynch, . .	1731	M.L.	133
Blanchard, James and Anne Martha Russell, .	1736	M.L.	123
Bladham, Cecilia and Walter Commons, .	1731	M.L.	110
Blundell, Sir Francis (Bart.) and Anne Ingoldsby, .	1676	M.L.	17
Bocchi, Lorenzo and Marjory Drury, . .	1729	M.L.	76
Bogle, Archibald and Lydia Pringle, widow, .	1713	M.L.	4
Boland, Martha and Benjamin Wells, . .	1737	M.L.	40
Bold, John and Elizabeth Hockon, . .	1729	M.L.	61
Bolland, Susannah and John Eaton, . .	1723	M.L.	23
Bolton, Anne and John Turner, . . .	1713	M.L.	3

CORRECTIONS, DUBLIN GRANT INDEX, 1372–1800—*continued*.

Name, Place, and Occupation.	Year.	Nature of Record.	Page.
Bond, Harry and Elizabeth Blackney,	1686	M.L.	4
„ Martha and George Clappann,	1734	M.L.	5
Boshell, Martin and Mary Lechford,	1713	M.L.	1
Bostwick, Philip and Rose Payne, widow,	1159	M.L.	6
Boteford, Mary and Maurice Nash,	1726	M.L.	3
Bonden, Mary and John Jones,	1680	M.L.	4
Boughert, Anne (widow) and William Jackson,	1681	M.L.	71
Boughton, Thomas and Martha Gladwell,	1722	M.L.	75
Boulgue, Simon and Perotte Mary Trulyet,	1737	M.L.	91
Bonnain, Lewis and Ann Muldonk,	1736	M.L.	27
Bourk, John and Elizabeth Piddock, widow,	1711	M.L.	17
Bourze, Richard and Jane Smith,	1708	M.L.	131
Bourrows, Mary and Michael Finey,	1739	M.L.	8
Boutsand, Margaret and Robert Deane,	1723	M.L.	15
Bowden, Samuel and Jane Medcum, widow,	1675	M.L.	12
Bowen, Elizabeth (widow) and John Luther,	1681	M.L.	21
Bowrie, Elizabeth and Benjamin Mead,	1681	M.L.	77
Boyne, George and Susan Miller,	1679	M.L.	6
Boyle, Bellingham and Sarah Hoadly,	1780	M.L.	141
Boyne, Frances and Nathaniel Radford,	1738	M.L.	141
Bradin, Robert (Rev.) and Henrietta Bioromo,	1671	M.L.	3
Bragge, Elizabeth and Henry Garred,	1679	M.L.	6
Braithwaite, Mary and Francis Hill,	1722	M.L.	129
Brennan, Rose (widow) and James Dunn,	1730	M.L.	86
Brundy, William and Jane Ward, widow,	1735	M.L.	5
Brannon, Judith and Peter Humaton,	1735	M.L.	131
Brazill, Elinor (widow) and Andrew Walton,	1733	M.L.	63
Braughtaridge, Hannah and John Daniel,	1731	M.L.	144
Breraly, James and Alle Moss,	1680	M.L.	61
„ James and Mary Thexton,	1680	M.L.	44
Brereton, Catherine and Edward Langham,	1675	M.L.	17
Brise, Eleanor and Patrick Skefe,	1671	M.L.	7
Brimsweede, Eliza and Joseph Butter,	1678	M.L.	3
Bringly, Margaret and Edward Webb,	1674	M.L.	6
Brinhall, Anne (widow) and Thomas Granger,	1671	M.L.	10
Brirts, Alexander and Jane Ennis,	1733	M.L.	38
Brimes, Patrick and Abigail Corker,	1700	M.L.	31
Bristo, Jane and John Clark,	1737	M.L.	63
Bristow, Jane and John Clark,	1773	M.L.	6

CORRECTIONS, DUBLIN GRANT INDEX, 1272-1800—continued.

Name, Place, and Occupation.	Year.	Nature of Record.	Page.
Bristow, Skeffington and Elizabeth Grattan,	1734	M.L.	63
Britt, Christopher and Catherine Beycoble,	1735	M.L.	97
Brittaine, George and Margaret Butlerion,	1673	M.L.	8
Britton, Mary (widow) and Roger Robins,	1738	M.L.	121
Brittan, Anne and Charles Nuttall,	1736	M.L.	131
Brook, Sarah and James Fade,	1693	M.L.	73
Bruff, Margaret (widow) and Richard Andrews,	1731	M.L.	113
Bruckes, Mary and Guy Carelton,	1713	M.L.	2
Brunks, Anne and Samuel Cottnam,	1733	M.L.	169
Brewmer, Henry and Mary Bradford,	1731	M.L.	116
„ John and Alice Barker,	1692	M.L.	52
Breeghall, Richard and Catherine Divin,	1674	M.L.	15
Bromly, Joseph and Bridget Burons,	1728	M.L.	2nd
Brown, Catherine Grace and Richard Hatfield,	1739	M.L.	66
„ Henry and Mary Earl,	1721	M.L.	38
„ Temperance and Charles Bagot,	1728	M.L.	64
Browne, John and Frances Jones,	1727	D.L.	160
„ Joseph and Jane King,	1738	M.L.	1
„ Margaret (widow) and Robert Denny,	1739	M L	34
„ Michael and Elinor Storl,	1737	M.L.	115
Bruston, Catherine and James Harrow,	1735	M.L.	103
Brumley, Thomas and Jane West,	1720	M.L.	130
Brunwich, Mary (widow) and Alexander Rigby,	1841	M.L.	62
Brummel, Samuel and Savannah Garrod,	1738	M.L.	205
Brunton, Richard and Anne Price,	1738	M.L.	184
„ or Brunton, William and Mary Nicholson,	1837	M.L.	20
Bryan, Lawrence and Mary Fottorall,	1731	M.L.	181
Bryer, Susannah and John Trelyn,	1738	M.J.	153
Bryne, Catherine and Garrett Redmund,	1684	M.L.	71
Buckeley, John and Mary Fisher,	1739	M.L.	35
Bucknall, Elizabeth and Meredith Gwillim,	1675	M.L.	14
Buistra, Jane (widow) and Paul Guimet,	1739	M.L.	38
Bulskley, Adrian and Sarah Allen, widow,	1734	M L	69
Bulkeley, Jane (widow) and Henry Bellwood,	1713	M.L.	3
Buly, Isabella and Kennedy Farrell,	1733	M.L.	63
Bunbury, Diana and Edward Ormack,	1733	M.L.	31
„ Hannah (widow) and George Kade,	1657	M.L.	84
„ Henry and Jane M'Clarin,	1736	M.L.	77
Burbridge, Eliza (widow) and Miles Ewbieth,	1681	M.L.	73

CORRECTIONS, DUBLIN GRANT INDEX, 1272–1800— *continued.*

Name. Place, and Occupation.	Year.	Nature of Record.	Page
Burchs, Peter and Sarah Morton, ...	1672	M.L.	1
Burleigh, Mary and Richard Cooke, . . .	1738	M.L.	10
Burgess, Mary and Henry Cleaver, . . .	1694	M.L.	72
Burnaby, John and Anne Courtney, . . .	.719	M.L.	18
Burnside, James and Dorise Bowles, . . .	1678	M.L.	5
Burstiane, Dorothy (widow) and William Swift, . .	1671	M.L.	1
Burre, Humphrey and Elizabeth Symons, . .	1684	M.L.	2
Burrel, Sarah and John Fletcher, . . .	1738	M.L.	12
Burton, Elizabeth and John Coyle, . . .	1711	M L.	12
— Mary (widow) and French Walsh, . . .	1730	M L.	18
Buss, Anne and Andibert Foure, ...	1728	M.L.	1
Busher, Helen and Mary Griffin, . . .	1723	M.L.	0
Buskell, Thomas and Rachel Blackhorne or blackthorne	1688	M.L.	4
Buteux, John and Madeleine Dejournart, . .	1730	M.L.	6
Butler, Charles and Elizabeth Balton, widow, .	1713	M L.	1
— Ignatius and Ellen Cullen, . . .	1728	M.L.	6
— James and Elizabeth Thomallasson, . .	1728	M.L.	28
— Mary and James M'Maughan, . . .	1737	M.L.	0
Butterton, Margaret and George Brittaine, . .	1673	M.L.	1
Byass, William and Elinor Lynch, . . .	1714	M.L.	11
Byrne, Elizabeth and Daniel Girard, . . .	1737	M.L.	163
— Henry and Diana Sheridan, widow, . .	1730	M.L.	2
— Martha and Richard Saunders, . . .	1738	M.L.	9
— Mary and Robert Jones, ...	1787	M.L.	18
— Mary and William Maleall, . . .	1710	M.L.	6
Cadwallader, Talitha and Charles Dard, . .	1730	M.L.	N
Cahill, Hugh and Mary Finn, . . .	1777	M.L.	183
Caius, Matthew (alias Darroney) and Elizabeth Hawkins, .	1676	M.L.	10
Caldoe, Elizabeth and William Dewatson, . .	1676	M.L.	9
Callan, Patrick and Catherine Moore, . . .	1718	M.L.	1
Calloner, Richard (or Challoner) and Margaret Flaughberry,	1677	M.L.	2
Callwell, Isabella and Dominick Lombard, . .	1678	M.L.	13
Camak, Elizabeth and William Moffett, . .	1734	M.L.	44
Campbel, Mary and John Wright, . . .	1738	M.L.	24
Campbell, Ralph and Elizabeth Allison, . .	1730	M L.	6
Canavan, Gabriel and Elizabeth Fanchuy, widow, .	1748	M.L.	6
Cann, Elizabeth and George Fraulx, . . .	1740	M.L.	18

CORRECTIONS, DUBLIN GRANT INDEX, 1372–1800—continued.

Name, Place, and Occupation.	Year.	Nature of Record.	Page.
Cass, Sarah and John Tasker,	1875	M.L.	17
Cassens, Patrick and Jane Allen, widow,	1724	M.L.	43
Casney, William and Isabella Dowson, widow,	1741	M.L.	177
Cast, Alice and James Park,	1710	M.L.	81
Castwell, John and Elizabeth Story, widow,	1710	M.L.	61
Casyam, Gerald and Grace Yeates, widow,	1789	M.L.	73
Caps, Mary and Charles Cassidy,	1740	M.L.	63
— Matthew and Ruth Barrett, widow,	1733	M.L.	123
Carbry, John and Hester Quin,	1883	M.L.	68
Card, Ralph and Mary Murrell, widow,	1777	M.L.	49
Cardes, Alice and William Emerson,	1840	M.L.	390
Carelton, Guy and Mary Brookes,	1713	M.L.	2
Carmoross, Elizabeth and John Cologan,	1737	M.L.	164
Carirles, George and Mary Harris, widow,	1730	M.L.	149
Cartils, Joseph and Anne M'Mullen,	1711	M.L.	137
Cormick, William and Elizabeth Dawson,	1759	M.L.	71
Carawall, John and Mary Clark,	1710	M.L.	63
Carpenter, William and Mary Raives,	1714	M.L.	16
Carricks, Simon and Phillis (otherwise Phellicia) White, widow,	1678	M.L.	5
Carten, William and Phœbe Crooks, widow,	1739	M.L.	61
Carter, Sarah and John Kelly,	1741	M.L.	113
Cartwright, Sarah Elizabeth and John Bartram L.	1737	M.L.	155
Carty, Charles and Chasy Johnson,	1874	M.L.	11A
Casey, Robert and Katherine Morris,	1736	M.L.	910
Casey, Oliver and Rowland Parker,	1731	M.L.	111
Cassidy, Charles and Mary Caps,	1740	M.L.	63
Castle, Richard and Jane Truffett,	1733	M.L.	81
Catherwood, John and Margaret Allmerry, widow,	1739	M.L.	328
Caufield, Terence and Elinor Bird,	1735	M.L.	69
Caussar, Robert and Elizabeth Colson,	1739	M.L.	83
Cauxar, Ann and Cyrus Jennin,	1741	M.L.	113
Cavallar, John Anthony and Elizabeth Margaret Du Fontier,	1714	M.L.	11
Caverd, Mary and George Taylor,	1681	M.L.	34
Cawthren, Peter and Bridget Allen,	1730	M.L.	100
Cayus, Joseph and Mary Blackmore,	1841	M.L.	76
Crary, Francis and Susannah Willsun, widow,	1710	M.L.	64
Calla, Judith and Paul Chandill,	1733	M.L.	114
Cowynick, Joyce and James Wallis,	1878	M.L.	27
Chalmour, William and Mary Mann, widow,	1880	M.L.	46A

CORRECTIONS, DUBLIN GRANT INDEX, 1272–1800 —*continued*.

CORRECTIONS, DUBLIN GRANT INDEX, 1272-1800—*continued*.

Name, Place, and Occupation.	Year.	Nature of Record.	Page.
Coghlan, Ellen and Foake Cumberford, .	1657	M.L.	91
„ Matthias and Elizabeth Hill, .	1739	M.L.	107
Cole, Elizabeth and Thomas Albritton, .	1759	M.L.	73
„ Frances and Thomas Domville, .	1654	M.L.	77
Coleman, John and Elizabeth Garretson,	1737	M.L.	104
Colton, Elizabeth and Robert Oacomr, .	1729	M.L.	85
Colville, Margaret and James Webster, .	1723	M.L.	120
Combe, Oscar and Rachel Seboul,	1737	M.L.	63
Cumberford, Foake and Ellen Coghlan, .	1657	M.L.	91
„ William and Martha Priest,	1677	M.L.	29
Cummins, Walter and Cecilia Bloxham, .	1721	M.L.	119
Contrell, Thomas and Susan Purvale, .	1717	M.L.	64
Conran, John and Mary Curran, .	1738	M.L.	77
Constable, Benjamin and Anne Maty, .	1777	M.L.	61
„ John and Susannah Stokes, .	1739	M.L.	60
Cook, Samuel and Judith Tresch,	1722	M.L.	40
Coole, Letitia and Robert Moodlesworth,	1675	M.L.	91
Cooley, Anne and Robert Perry, .	1729	M.L.	103
„ Rebecca and Robert Atkin, .	1672	M.L.	3
„ Thomas and Mary Dullahannty, .	1683	M.L.	58
Cooper, Catherine (widow) and William Eliott,	1680	M.L.	61
Cope, Christiana and Thomas Delemaun,	1729	M.L.	223
Cordiner, Jane and James Woodside, .	1733	M.L.	121
Corker, Abigail and Patrick Briscoe, .	1718	M.L.	81
„ Edward and Prudence Jenkins, .	1700	M.L.	65
Cornwall, Elizabeth and Hugh Bignall, .	1683	M.L.	70
Corran, Elizabeth and Francis Mallit, .	1741	M.L.	211
Corrigan, Patrick and Margaret M'Quaad.	1741	M.L.	108
Currill, Elizabeth and Joshua Kember, .	1729	M.L.	25
Corris, Thomas and Jane Cutler, .	1731	M.L.	81
Corry, Henry and Catherine Langon, .	1741	M.L.	181
Corrys, Anne and Michael Cheeps, .	1739	M.J.	89
Corvin, Manuel and Mary Middleton, .	1714	M.L.	11
Cosby, Francis and Judith Piggott, .	1733	M.L.	29
Cotter, Jane and Thomas Corris, .	1731	M.L.	44
Cottgrave, Catherine and Robert Boasier.	1663	M.L.	72
Cottingham, James and Elizabeth Deacy, .	1676	M.L.	12
Cottnam, Eliza (alias Charpless), widow, and Solomon Le Merchand.	1671	M.L.	31
„ Mary Anne and Edward Whitehead, .	1738	M.L.	203

CORRECTIONS, DUBLIN GRANT INDEX, 1272–1800—continued.

Name, Place, and Occupation.	Year.	Nature of Record.	Page.
Cottnam, Samuel and Anne Brooks, ...	1785	M.L.	139
Cougf, Mary and Paul Tanner, ...	1727	M.L.	62
Coughlan, John and Clara Gormely, ...	1680	M.L.	21
Coault, John and Sarah Carr, ...	1730	M.L.	23
_ Robert and Sarah Riely, ...	1733	M.L.	23
Countess, John and Susan Grimsuit, ...	1689	M.L.	55
Courtney, Anne and John Bournsby, ...	1710	M.L.	91
Cox, Elizabeth (widow) and Bernard Wayte, . .	1682	M.L.	61
Coxe, Shem and Rachel Rutter, ...	1677	M.L.	27
Coyle, John and Elizabeth Burton, ...	1741	M.L.	123
_ Nicholas and Margaret Keehan, . .	1729	M.L.	65
Crampton, John and Dorothy Price, widow, . .	1727	M.L.	132
Cranfield, Dorcas and James Hart, ...	1728	M.L.	8
Crawley, Jeremiah and Mary Hammon, widow, .	1738	M.L.	132
Cregge, Sarah and Jonathan Walker, ...	1734	M.L.	61
Creagh, Margaret and Marcus-James Kennedy, .	1731	M.L.	130
Creichtonne, Amelia and Henry Leslie, . .	1741	M.L.	149
Creighton, Elizabeth and Hugh Hammill, . .	1873	M.L.	9
Cremen, William and Ellnor Petitt, ...	1684	M.L.	71
Cripe, Marjory (widow) and Charles Hendrick, .	1720	M.L.	55
Crenkford, John and Penelope Housdall, widow, .	1678	M.L.	9
Cronin, Andrew and Mary Lyon, ...	1741	M.L.	136
Crooke, Phebe (widow) and William Carson, .	1729	M.L.	61
Crosby, Daniel and Margaret Moran, ...	1727	M.L.	149
_ John and Mary Thompson, ...	1729	M.L.	114
Cross, Peter and Rachel Rentwert, ...	1728	M.L.	55
Creahoo, John and Elizabeth Cronna, ...	1677	M.L.	27
Cross, Richard and Mary Dyer widow, . .	1711	M.L.	13
Crowder, Anne and Andrew Engelhart, . .	1740	M.L.	77
Cruckly, Sarah and John Walls, ...	1680	M.L.	44
Crumpe, George and Elizabeth Whitehead, widow, .	1680	M.L.	8
Culbert, Joseph and Elinor Horton, ...	1733	M.L.	61
Callam, Deborah and Henry Hosyer, . .	1681	M.L.	61
Cullen, Ellen and Ignatius Butler, ...	1729	M.L.	67
Cumpkin, James and Mary Mealor, ...	1788	M.L.	132
Cuningham, Andrew and Anne Reed, . .	1729	M.L.	8
Cuppaidge, Elizabeth and Samuel Gleadowe, .	1720	M.L.	149
Curlett, Anne and Edward Watkins, ...	1728	M.L.	209
Curron, Magdalene and Charles Le Maistret, .	1673	M.L.	8

CORRECTIONS, DUBLIN GRANT INDEX, 1273–1800—*continued.*

Name, Place, and Description.	Year.	Nature of Record.	Page.
Cusack, Edward and Diana Barahory, . . .	1732	M.I.	51
„ Elinor and Simon Archbold, . . .	1671	M.I.	8
„ William and Susannah Morgan, widow, .	1741	M.I.	105
Cuthbert, William and Catherine Newcombe, widow,	1671	M.I.	16
Cavilles, John and Mary M'Glann, . . .	1723	M.I.	6
Cavillis, James and Elizabeth Walton, . . .	1738	M.I.	103
Daly, Miles and Anne Braughall, . . .	1737	M.I.	62
Banot, William and Anne Howriah, . . .	1738	M.I.	113
Baskell, Samuel and Charlotte Magdalene Catherine Beaumont.	1710	M.I.	98
Dugros, John and Margaret Prior, . . .	1733	M.I.	108
Darby, Ambrosia Edgworth and Rathborne Mills, .	1740	M.I.	62
Barry, Charles and Henrietta Goodricke, . .	1740	M.I.	70
Davvy, Sarah and Charles Howison, . . .	1723	M.I.	67
Bevian, Elizabeth and George Williams, . .	1723	M.I.	6
„ John and Rebecca Ashmanbry, . . .	1726	M.I.	101
Davia, Henry and Anne Mack, . . .	1720	M.I.	64
Davison, William and Elizabeth M'Dright, widow, .	1730	M.I.	70
Dawson, Elizabeth and William Garmick, . .	1729	M.I.	71
„ James and Jane Rogers, . . .	1678	M.I.	16
„ Sarah and Joseph Allcross, . . .	1731	M.I.	100
„ Walter and Catherine Grattan, . .	1741	M.L.	123
Bay, Elizabeth and John Harris, . . .	1713	M.I.	70
Dealy, John and Dorothy King, . . .	1729	M.I.	93
Buxma, Robert and Margaret Boatsand, . .	1731	M.I.	117
De Bacquancourt, *see* Des Voeux.			
Debrumacal, Charlotte Magdalene Catherine and Samuel Dalell	1738	M.I.	85
Beasy, Peter and Hester Hiscock, . . .	1749	M.I.	193
Decombe, Jane and Richard Shorter, . . .	1735	M.I.	34
De Dewrdilly, Anne and John Dunscall, . .	1683	M.I.	69
De Favre, James and Pauline Viella, . . .	1714	M.I.	19
Dejemevart, Madelaine and John Buianx, . .	1730	M.I.	42
Dallanvest, Thomas and Christiana Coto, . .	1743	M.I.	101
Beauxi, William and Margaret Falvey, . .	1776	M.L.	50
Denny, Margaret and William Munson, junior, .	1772	M.L.	168
Depennaire, James and Elizabeth Waller, . .	1657	M.I.	61
Deyrular, John and Louisa Armourand, widow, .	1733	M.L.	27
Barvy, Catherine and Pierce Moore, . . .	1741	M.I.	128

CORRECTIONS, DUBLIN GRANT INDEX, 1272–1800—*continued*.

Name, Place, and Occupation.	Year.	Nature of Record.	Page.
Derragh, John and Mary Tysart, widow,	1730	M.L.	203
Derrenzy, Matthew (alias Gaine) and Elizabeth Hawkins,	1670	M.L.	19
Derry, Nathaniel and Anne Gouldsmith,	1670	M.L.	23
De Sally, Jane and David Paine,	1730	M.L.	166
Desmyniers, Easter and Edmund Birmingham,	1740	M.L.	94
Destarre, Catharine and Heyolrich Von Krayn Mirckes,	1683	M.L.	8
De Bury, Sophie Magdeiro and Rev. John Mary Vernenil,	1 27	M.L.	161
De Bury, Alexander and Louisa Adée,	1711	M.L.	18
Des Vœux (de Bacquancourt), Rev. Marie Anthony Vicherablo Vitohau and Mary Louise Querqui (de Challais),	1730	M.L.	107
Devenish, William and Elizabeth Blake, widow,	1730	M.L.	61
Deys, Rose (or Dyes), widow, and Daniel Carroll,	1676	M.L.	21
Delmonhes, Isaac an t Eliner Tyrrell,	1735	M.L.	171
Dick, John and Mary Melhuish,	1740	M.L.	61
Diskinson, John and Savannah Hells,	1749	M.L.	81
Dickinson, James and Elizabeth Gartagar, widow,	1737	M.L.	177
Dillan, Elinor (widow) and John Hodgson,	1737	M.L.	164
,, Mary and Peter Weston,	1675	M.L.	17
Diodariel, Joseph and Elizabeth Godfrey,	1730	M.L.	29
Dissey, Robert and Margaret Browne, widow,	1789	M.L.	91
Ditchfield, John and Catharine M'Hitterick, widow,	1735	M.L.	81
Divon, James and Catharine Sutton,	1631	M.L.	14
Divis, Catherine and Richard Broughall,	1676	M.L.	23
Dobar, John and Alice Howard,	1680	M.L.	61
Dobson, Anne and Rev. William Tryddic,	1737	M.L.	18
,, Vincent and Elizabeth Shelvin	1679	M.L.	8
Dodd, Margaret and Thomas Glanton,	1738	M.L.	21
Dodson, George and Susan Squire,	1780	M.L.	161
,, Thomas and Mary Fleetwood,	1683	M.L.	8
Dogherty, Frances and Marlborough Sterling,	1735	M.L.	73
Dunville, Thomas and Frances Cole,	1634	M.L.	7
Donvill, Lucy and William Mollosux,	1670	M.L.	8
Donalan, John and Elizabeth Aston, widow,	1676	M.L.	11
Donellan, Edmund and Dorothy Busers,	1673	M.L.	4
Donnelly, Deborah (widow) and Thomas Ellis,	1734	M.L.	9
Donnellan, John and Hannah Gore,	1737	M.L.	9
Dooly (or Dooty), Dorothy and Matthew Quan, widow,	1676	M.L.	9
Doran, Catharine and Daniel Sharp,	1731	M.L.	16
Dowdall, Lancelot and Elizabeth Jones,	1719	M.L.	9

CORRECTIONS, DUBLIN GRANT INDEX, 1972-1800—continued.

Name, Place, and Occupation.	Year.	Nature of Record.	Page.
Dowdall, Patrick and Mary Hand,	1731	M.L.	177
„ Richard and Anne Murphy, widow,	1736	M.L.	145
Dowell, Edward and Elizabeth Wolseley,	1711	M.L.	131
Dowglass, Jane and George Sturgeon,	1734	M.L.	44
Downey, Michael and Jane Ponder,	1739	M.L.	46
Dorwon, Isabella (widow) and William Cancey,	1741	M.L.	197
Drinkwater, Dorothy and Richard Wildman,	1682	M.L.	63
Driskell, Elinor and George Rose,	1732	M.L.	130
Deams, Catherine and Thomas Merdith,	1738	M.L.	197
Dallahunty, Mary and Thomas Cooley,	1682	M.L.	64
Damn U, John and Anne De Dourdilly,	1673	M.L.	68
Danboig, Jane and Solomon Leblanc,	1721	M.L.	24
Dunlap, Andrew and Sarah Sealy,	1733	M.L.	20
Dunn, James and Rose Brennan, widow,	1736	M.L.	100
„ William and Sarah Robison,	1741	M.L.	131
Du Feurier, Elizabeth Margaret and John Anthony Cavalier,	1714	M.L.	11
Dupay, Hester and Charles Mercier,	1713	M.L.	31
„ John and Frances Gantier,	1739	M.L.	124
Dussais, Samuel and Margaret Harel,	1728	M.L.	196
Deismal, John and Martha Hemming,	1737	M.L.	175
Devell, Mary (widow) and Christopher Shannon,	1778	M.L.	819
Dyer, Mary (widow) and Richard Cross,	1711	M.L.	19
Earl, Mary and Henry Brown,	1728	M.L.	35
„ Rooke and Margaret White,	1729	M.L.	69
Eaton, Elizabeth (widow) and (George) Morgan,	1714	M.L.	10
Eaton, Jane and Edmund Colton,	1673	M.L.	16
Eckle, James and Mary Anne Sampson,	1729	M.L.	19
Edmerely, Thomasina (widow) and Caleb Noreth,	1729	M.L.	90
Edmunds, William and Jane Pierce,	1783	M.L.	41
Edwards, Hannah (widow) and John Hill,	1739	M.L.	85
„ Mary and Matthew Tenson,	1743	M.L.	136
„ Oswald and Ellenbeth M Call,	1730	M.L.	100
Eelm, Mary and John Martin,	1737	M.L.	170
Eglia, John and Mary Mitchell,	1728	M.L.	35
Eliza, Hester and Edward Warters,	1723	M.L.	4
Elder, Elizabeth and John M'Connell,	1741	M.L.	125
Edington, William and Grace Glass,	1677	M.L.	23

CORRECTIONS, DUBLIN GRANT INDEX, 1272-1800—*continued*.

Name, Place, and Occupation.	Year.	Nature of Record.	Page.
Ellurs, Elizabeth and John Scott,	1731	M.L.	6
Elliot, Elizabeth and Thomas Hitchings,	1713	M.L.	7
Ellis, Joan and Peter Kelly,	1713	M.L.	2
„ Thomas and Deborah Donolly, widow,	1734	M.L.	6
„ William and Mary Mosley, widow,	1739	M.L.	5
Ellison, William and Anne Hoper,	1716	M.L.	13
Elrington, Mary and William Hall,	1741	M.L.	108
Elsey, Martin and Elizabeth Clenchey, widow,	1723	M.L.	9
Eltoft, William and Catherine Cooper, widow,	1690	M.L.	6
Emer, Richard and Susan Harris,	1689	M.L.	17
Emer, Philip and Anne Lefahon,	1722	M.L.	6
Empson, Charles and Mary Mathers, widow,	1673	M.L.	1
Engelhart, Andrew and Anne Crowder,	1729	M.L.	11
Ennis, Jane and Alexander Belvin,	1729	M.L.	28
Enfill, Margaret and Anselm Ince,	1741	M.L.	18
Easington, Rebecca and John Fisher,	1739	M.L.	17
Eustace, Catherine and James Peppard Warren,	1726	M.L.	9
„ Maurice and Elizabeth Pelin,	1655	M.L.	6
Evans, Henry and Mary Birkett,	1690	M.L.	7
Eveleigh, Miles and Ellen Burbridge,	1654	M.L.	13
Everard, Benjamin and Henrietta Wakely,	1736	M.L.	16
Everet, John and Deborah Allen,	1729	M.L.	1
Evay, William and Hannah Plumar,	1677	M.L.	2
Ewer, Thomas and Elizabeth Lawrence, widow,	1624	M.L.	11
Fade, James and Sarah Brook,	1683	M.L.	13
Falcumburye, Joachim and Anne Tadpole,	1683	M.L.	6
Falkner, George and Mary Gruby,	1741	M.L.	15
Falvey, Margaret and William Dexall,	1785	M.L.	8
Fann, John and Elizabeth Phipps,	1730	M.L.	12
Fanning, Edward (Rev.) and Joanna French,	1783	M.L.	13
Faryhor, Charles and Anne Laros,	1716	M.L.	1
Farrel, Francis and Catherine Slattin,	1738	M.L.	19
Farrall, Edmundy and Isabella Buly,	1769	M.L.	6
Fart, James and Mary Ball,	1714	M.L.	11
Faushesy, Elizabeth (widow) and Gabriel Camran,	1716	M.L.	8
Faulkner, Rebecca and John Reddy,	1727	M.L.	6
Feare, Andibert and Anne Buse,	1739	M.L.	94

CORRECTIONS, DUBLIN GRANT INDEX, 1272–1600—*continued.*

CORRECTIONS. DUBLIN GRANT INDEX, 1272–1800—*continued.*

Name, Place, and Occupation.	Year.	Nature of Record.	Page.
Fox, Daniel and Margaret Ferrall,	1713	M.L.	1
„ Jerh and Elizabeth Story,	1726	M.L.	2
„ Walter and Mary Strafford, widow,	1737	M.L.	6
Foxton, Marmaduke and Elizabeth Worthy, widow,	1681	M.L.	4
Foy, John and Mary Jacolin Prideur,	1673	M.L.	1
Fraines, Esther and Hugh Kerr,	1728	M.L.	6
Fraiser, Thomas and Anne Goffe, widow,	1715	M.L.	2
Franelm, Elizabeth and Henry Hilton,	1676	M.L.	6
Freeman, Richard and Elinor Hutton,	1715	M.L.	2
French, Elizabeth and James Low,	1678	M.L.	6
„ James and Anne Godfrey,	1735	M.L.	2
„ Joanna and Rev. Edward Fanning,	1733	M.L.	5
Prideur, Mary Jacolin and John Foy,	1673	M.L.	1
Furama, Edith and James Marten,	1734	M.L.	6
Gadis, John and Mary Turaly,	1784	M.L.	6
Gaulter, Frances and John Dupuy,	1723	M.L.	26
Gardiner, Edward and Jane Grace,	1725	M.L.	3
Garsecbe, Isac and Daniel Onion,	1737	M.L.	6
Garnett, Elizabeth and Henry Kinkead,	1739	M.L.	8
„ Mary and William Battersby, junior,	1735	M.L.	120
„ Mary and Moses Marcum,	1680	M.L.	4
Garrett, Mary (widow) and John Wade,	1741	M.L.	122
Garrod, Henry and Elizabeth Bragee,	1676	M.L.	6
Garstin, Mary and John Conran,	1736	M.L.	77
Gaudy, Peter and Jane Wall,	1675	M.L.	114
Gauxter, Jane and Francis Begus,	1685	M.L.	78
Gedges, George and Sophia Jemerson,	1716	M.L.	6
Gental, Peter and Mary Morean,	1716	M.L.	6
Geoghegan, Elizabeth (widow) and Dennis Wedgworth,	1725	M.L.	6
George, Dennis and Sarah Young, widow,	1736	M.L.	143
Gihall, Sarah and James Taylor,	1731	M.L.	103
Gibson, Anne Spencer and Robert Jones,	1723	M.L.	6
„ Matthew and Elizabeth Casey,	1729	M.L.	76
Girard, Daniel and Elizabeth Byrne,	1737	M.L.	146
Gladwell, Martha and Thomas Boughton,	1723	M.L.	3
Glannan, Thomas and Margaret Dodd,	1739	M.L.	127
Glanvill, Robert and Abigail Marrobie,	1739	M.L.	128

CORRECTIONS, DUBLIN GRANT INDEX, 1272–1800—*continued.*

Name, Place, and Occupation.	Time.	Nature of Record.	Page.
Giuse, Grace and William Elliagaton, ...	1677	M.L.	19
Glandows, Samuel and Elizabeth Cuppaidge, .	1738	M.L.	164
Godfrey, George and Susannah Olifford, . .	1710	M.L.	67
Goffe, Anne (widow) and Thomas Frazier, . .	1713	M.L.	73
Goggin, Martha and Henry Combes. . .	1741	M.L.	130
Golborne, Elizabeth and William Hamill, . .	1671	M.L.	6
Golding, Andrew and Margaret Smith, . . .	1729	M.L.	71
Gonne, Rebecca and John Harper, . . .	1735	M.L.	87
Good, Elizabeth and John Walter, . . .	1723	M.L.	68
Goodbody, Samuel and Elinor M'Collister, . .	1735	M.L.	101
Goodlass, John and Elizabeth Kenny, . .	1791	M.L.	85
Goodriske, Harriatta and Charles Darcy, .	1740	M.L.	79
Goodwin, Frances and David M'Ginty, . .	1731	M.L.	118
Gordan, Samuel and Grace Bermaford, . . .	1727	M.L.	41
Gore, Hannah and John Donnellan, . . .	1777	M.L.	61
Gormaly, Clara and John Coughlan, . . .	1069	M.L.	60
Gormley, John and Margaret Bathoe, . . .	1672	M.L.	87
Gorrnah, Mabel and George Nolan, . . .	1735	M.L.	87
Gouldsmith, Anne and Nathaniel Derry, . .	1670	M.L.	11
Govers, John and Elizabeth Belm, widow, .	1735	M.L.	173
Grass, Gerald and Anne Kiernan, . . .	1671	M.L.	90
„ Jane and Edward Gardiner, . . .	1735	M.L.	93
„ Susannah and William Marksfeld, .	1732	M.L.	40
Grantwood, Sarah (widow) and William Rathbone, .	1738	M.L.	159
Graham, Anne and James Baker, . . .	1654	M.L.	14
Granger, Thomas and Anne Bristnall (widow), .	1674	M.L.	16
Grattan, Catherine and Walter Dawson, . .	1741	M.L.	167
„ Elizabeth and Skeffington Bristow, . .	1734	M.L.	53
Graves, Elinor (widow) and Thomas Perry, .	1727	M.L.	177
Gravill, John and Hannah Halpen, . .	1740	M.L.	168
„ Mary (or Granvill) and John Carmichael, . .	1723	M.L.	23
Gray, A—— (widow) and Donal O'Brien, .	1671	M.L.	67
Grayden, Catherine and William Ormsby, . .	1733	M.L.	74
Green, Edward and Mary Ormerod, widow, .	1717	M.L.	61
„ Frances and Anthony Chapman, . .	1709	M.L.	99
Gregan, Elizabeth and John Croaker, . .	1677	M.L.	27
Gregory, Bridget and Daniel May, . .	1727	M.L.	36
Greenwood, Jane (widow) and John Hamilton, .	1678	M.L.	75
Greenway, William and Elizabeth Alab, . .	1729	M.L.	63

CORRECTIONS, DUBLIN GRANT INDEX, 1272-1800—*continued.*

Name, Place, and Occupation.	Year.	Nature of Record.	Page.
Grely, John and Margaret Dodd, ...	1673	M.L.	5
Grevell, John and Susan Swinfield, ...	1681	M.L.	6
Griffin, Mary and Robert Bashaw, ...	1789	M.L.	8
Grimsault, Susan and John Comstone, . . .	1680	M.L.	6
Grindon, John and Margaret Vessel, . . .	1721	M.L.	10
Grinsall, Susannah (widow) and Rev. John Walker,	1730	M.L.	10
Grisewood, Mark and Sarah Simpson, . .	1767	M.L.	5
Grooms, Margaret and Thomas Larkin, . . .	1677	M.L.	1
Grosvenor, Sharington and Mary Winckworth, .	1673	M.L.	9
Gruby, Mary and George Falkner, . . .	1741	M.L.	16
Grumley, Benjamin and Jane Morris, . . .	1733	M.L.	26
Grumly, Cecily and Barnaby Tew, . . .	1740	M.L.	72
Guerry, Paul and Catharine Jones, . . .	1767	M.L.	45
Guest, Henry and Mary Parviesia, widow, . .	1731	M.L.	10
„ Thomas and Elizabeth Sullivan, widow, .	1738	M.L.	41
Guinet, Anne and Peter Rougier, . . .	1733	M.L.	5
„ Jane and Thomas Walker, . . .	1737	M.L.	8
„ Paul and Jane Bulmer, widow, .	1726	M.L.	8
„ Sarah (widow) and John Walker, . .	1737	M.L.	70
Guinet, Paul and Mary Harvey, widow, . .	1738	M.L.	111
Guion, Daniel and Jane Garmohe, . .	1777	M.L.	4
Gullaford, John and Marjery Pennington, widow, .	1677	M.L.	8
Gulston, Alice and John Fisher, . . .	1684	M.L.	71
Gunton, Benjamin and Elizabeth Harpitt, . .	1731	M.L.	13
Gwillim, Meredith and Elizabeth Bucknall, . .	1675	M.L.	1
Gwithur, Priscilla and James Richyson, . .	1744	M.L.	4
Gythen, Jane and George Hyde, ...	1739	M.L.	5
Hack, John of Wicresos, ...	1611	O.W.	—
Hackett, James and Belindly Barrel, . . .	1725	M.L.	10
Haggan, Denis and Martha Lewis, . . .	1737	M.L.	17
Haigo, James (or Haigo) and Hester Seawell, .	1683	M.L.	6
Hale, Mary and James Mills, ...	1738	M.L.	13
Halfpenny, Catharine and Ralph Chittchly, . .	1735	M.L.	5
Halgan, Christopher and Dorothy Uplinggohacas, widow,	1683	M.L.	8
Hall, William and Mary Charleton, . . .	1740	M.L.	9
„ William and Mary Errington, . .	1741	M.L.	13
Halpen, Hannah and John Gravil, . . .	1740	M.L.	16

CORRECTIONS, DUBLIN GRANT INDEX, 1272–1800—*continued.*

Name, Place, and Occupation.	Year.	Nature of Record.	Page.
Ham, Mary (widow) and James Arbuckle,	1729	M.L.	60
Hamill, William and Elizabeth Golborne,	1674	M.L.	6
Hamilton, Mary and Christopher Reilly,	1729	M.L.	64
Hamilton, Arabella Susan (Lady) and Sir John M'Gill,	1860	M.L.	69
„ Charles and Deborah Jowlan,	1731	M.L.	116
„ Francis and Lady Catherine Montgomery,	1656	M.L.	91
„ John and Jane Greenewood, widow,	1679	M.L.	13
„ Margaret Cecil and Hon. Thomas George Southwell,	1741	M.L.	123
Hammill, Hugh and Elizabeth Creighton,	1673	M.L.	5
Hampson, Mary (widow) and Jeremiah Crawley,	1729	M.L.	221
Hammond, Thomas and Margaret Sherman, widow,	1718	M.L.	29
Hanbidge, John and Mary Young,	1741	M.L.	149
Hand, Mary and Patrick Dowdall,	1738	M.L.	177
Handcock, Elizabeth and Cornelius Hughes,	1733	M.L.	24
Handisby, Mary and James Walmsly,	1739	M.L.	33
Hankinson, Elizabeth and John Tyler,	1739	M.L.	61
Hanlon, Sarah and William Balick,	1683	N.L.	61
Hardin, James and Elizabeth Lester,	1737	M.L.	67
Hardwick, James and Eden Massey,	1725	M.L.	38
Harivard, Peter and Joan Fitzgerald,	1726	M.L.	31
Harman, Jane and John Smith, junior,	1729	M.L.	66
„ Margaret and George Ivis,	1741	M.L.	159
Harmon, Mary and Sir Arthur Jones, knight,	1674	M.L.	16
Harper, Ctna (widow) and Joseph Allcock,	1709	M.L.	64
„ John and Rebecca Coome,	1734	M.L.	63
Harpiri, Elizabeth and Benjamin Gussow,	1781	M.L.	130
Harrington, Mary and William Mymara,	1677	M.L.	28
Harris, Mary (widow) and George Carleton,	1730	M.L.	100
„ Mary and John Haslocko,	1673	M.L.	4
„ Susan and Richard Eupor,	1683	M.L.	67
Harrison, Elizabeth and George Trim,	1737	M.L.	143
Harrobin, Abigail and Robert Glascril,	1736	M.L.	121
Harrow, James and Catherine Bruston,	1728	M.L.	193
Hartley, John and Margaret Minalti,	1737	M.L.	176
Hartliff, Frances and Joseph Agill,	1740	M.L.	83
Hartson, James and Charlotte Mary Chapell,	1731	M.L.	112
„ Sarah and Peter Wainwright,	1739	M.L.	86
Harvey, John and Elizabeth Day,	1723	M.L.	90
„ Mary (widow) and Paul Goinet,	1729	M.L.	116

CONNECTIONS, DUBLIN GRANT INDEX, 1272–1800—*continued*

Name, Place, and Occupation.	Year.	Nature of Record.	Page.
Harvis, Thomas and Eleanor Banks, widow, . . .	1672	M.L.	6
Haslocks, John and Mary Harris. . . .	1673	M.L.	6
Hatch, Nicholas and Mary Pullin. . . .	1678	M.L.	31
Hatcher, Frances (widow) and Joseph Revo. .	1677	M.L.	32
Hatchman, Martha and Christopher Healy, . .	1681	M.L.	64
Hatfield, Richard and Catherine Grace Brown. .	1720	M.L.	42
Hattam, Mary and Thomas Turner. . . .	1737	M.L.	146
Hatton, Francis and Mary Norris, . . .	1716	M.L.	31
Hatton, Elinor and Richard Freeman. . .	1728	M L.	77
Hawkins, Elizabeth and Matthew Derrecry *alias* Oaloe, .	1676	M.L.	13
Hawkins, Jane and James Thurgood. . .	1673	M.L.	11
Healy, John and Mary Bullick, widow, . .	1683	M.L.	73
Heatly, Charles and Jane Archerulby, . .	1740	M.L.	79
„ Isaac and Mary Berry, . . .	1731	M.L.	111
Hechstetter, Eliza and Richard Colack, . .	1680	M.L.	6
Helge, James (or Halge) and Hester Seawell, .	1683	M.L.	6
Hells, Susannah and John Dickinson, . .	1730	M.L.	43
Helme, John and Hannah Travers, widow, .	1711	M.L.	13
Hemming, Martha and John Dalrrel, . .	1737	M.L.	116
Hendrick, Charles and Margery Orim, widow, .	1700	M.L.	6
Henly, Jane and Michael Beaver, . . .	1734	M.L.	123
Hemhall, Richard and Mary Highmuroy. .	1737	M.L.	144
Hemill, Alice and Elijah Charles. . .	1714	M.L.	14
Herns, James and Jane Jones, . . .	1683	M.L.	64
Harrell, Frances and John Bonilla, . .	1714	M.L.	13
Hewetson, Michael and Lucy Vigors, . .	1722	M.L.	65
„ William and Elizabeth Oakley, .	1676	M.L.	6
Higgins, John and Elizabeth Perry, . .	1773	M.L.	103
Hill, Elizabeth and Matthias Coghlan, . .	1739	M.L.	167
„ Francis and Mary Braithwaite. . .	1729	M.L.	109
„ George and Elizabeth Latham, . .	1729	M.L.	6
„ John and Hannah Edwards, widow, .	1759	M.L.	63
„ Sarah and Andrew Mills, . . .	1730	M.L.	103
Hilman, Thomas and Joan M'Guckin, . .	1678	M.L.	14
Hilton, Henry and Elizabeth Frances, . .	1676	M.L.	6
Hindsman, Elinor and William Forsith, . .	1711	M L.	67
Hixms, Rebecca and Thomas Knight, . .	1716	M.L.	13
Hitchings, Thomas and Elizabeth Billot. .	1713	M.L.	7
Hoadly, Sarah and Bellingham Boyle, . .	1710	M.L.	68

CORRECTIONS, DUBLIN GRANT INDEX, 1272–1800—continued.

Name, Place, and Occupation.	Year.	Nature of Record.	Page.
Hobbs, Roger and Margaret Conner, widow,	1731	M.L.	135
Hodgson, John and Elinor Dillon, widow,	1737	M.L.	154
Holmes, Mary and William Phillipson,	1738	M.L.	161
Holmes, Robert (Rev.) and Jane Ball,	1758	M.L.	184
Holt, Mary and John Manson,	1728	M.L.	105
Hooks, Anne and Edward Dogly,	1677	M.L.	74
Hoakes, Elizabeth and John Hold,	1730	M.L.	61
Hooper, Henry and Deborah Cullam,	1682	M.L.	62
Hord, Anne and Samuel Clark,	1777	M.L.	68
Horish, Frances and William Swan,	1730	M.L.	104
— James and Mary Ann La Vigne,	1741	M.L.	115
Hornby, William and Rebecca Whitly,	1759	M.L.	16
Horridge, Anne and James Tuta,	1784	M.L.	67
Horton, Elinor and Joseph Cudbert,	1759	M.L.	68
— Mary and Edward Riley,	1575	M.L.	18
Houlton, James and Elinor Birch,	1757	M.L.	152
— John and Mary Lynch,	1730	M.L.	109
Housdell, Penelope (widow) and John Crockford,	1676	M.L.	63
Howard, Alice and John Dobar,	1680	M.L.	66
Howell, Joseph and Mary Ales,	1683	M.L.	86
Howison, Charles and Sarah Davey,	1728	M.L.	77
Howrish, Anne and William Dance,	1720	M.L.	111
Huband, Edmond and Elizabeth White, widow,	1738	M.L.	110
Hubbartsy, Mary and Richard Ramshall,	1737	M.L.	144
Hagginson, Frances and Sebastian Scrogie,	1730	M.L.	160
Hughes, Cornelius and Elizabeth Handcock,	1733	M.L.	84
— Owen and Elinor Parry,	1671	M.L.	5
Hughs, Hugh and Elizabeth Medlicott,	1739	M.L.	59
— William and Anne Shaw,	1759	M.L.	74
Humfrey, John and Sitella Spring,	1738	M.L.	110
Hanston, Peter and Judith Brunson,	1737	M.L.	621
Hunt, Anne and William Ellison,	1749	M.T.	75
— Dorothy and George Deddiess,	1677	M.L.	20
Hunter, John and Elizabeth Wilkinson,	1733	M.L.	128
Harvi, George and Jane West,	1757	M.L.	99
Hart, Frances and Joseph Chafin,	1671	M.L.	7
Husband, Benjamin and Elizabeth Abbott,	1730	M.L.	149
Hutchinson, Gilbert and Elizabeth Baldwin,	1676	M.L.	94
Hutchinson, Rachel (widow) and Thomas Inglefield,	1683	M.L.	64

CORRECTIONS, DUBLIN GRANT INDEX, 1272–1800—*continued*

Name, Place, and Occupation.	Year.	Nature of Record.	Page.
Hyde, George and Jane Clythes, ...	1739	M.L.	11
„ Margaret and William Ballard, ...	1789	M.L.	141
Ince, Austin and Margaret Endill, ...	1741	M.L.	119
Ingham, John and Jane Robinson, ...	1730	M.L.	13
Inglefield, Thomas and Rachel Hutchinson, widow.	1681	M.L.	44
Ingoldsby, Angelica and Robert, Earl of Roscommon, .	1718	M.L.	89
„ Agne and Sir Francis Blundell, bart. .	1671	M.L.	77
Iredall, Thomas and Margaret Agus, ...	1711	M.L.	16
Irwyn, Mary and John Norcott, ...	1789	M.L.	29
Isaac, John and Anne Ashenhurst, ...	1674	M.L.	6
Ivers, Anguwin and Susannah Rice, widow, . .	1781	M.L.	29
Ivie, George and Margaret Harman, ...	1741	M.L.	109
„ James and Christiana Bellwonal, . . .	1169	M.L.	8
Jackson, James and Jane M'Watlin, ...	1739	M.L.	115
„ John and Abigail Abidia, ...	1673	M.L.	1
„ Xodab and Elizabeth Searie, . . .	1734	M.L.	9
„ Mary (widow) and Thomas Silborck, . .	1729	M.L.	51
„ William and Anne Bourbart, widow, . .	1684	M.L.	77
Jacob, Mary and Walter May, ...	1673	M.L.	8
Jago, Elinor and John Lecar, ...	1739	M.L.	8
Janain, Cyrus and Ann Quarar, ...	1741	M.L.	115
Jennerun, Sophia and George Gedges, . . .	1740	M.L.	86
Jummalt, Frances and Henry Fisher, . . .	1729	M.L.	17
Jenkin, Thomas and Margaret Grumm, . .	1677	M.L.	21
Jenkins, Prudence and Edward Corker, . . .	1760	M.L.	6
„ William and Sarah Paine, ...	1741	M.L.	112
Johnson, Cicily and Charles Carty, . . .	1671	M.L.	111
„ William and Hannah Patrison, . . .	1789	M.L.	1
Johnston, Millicent and Richard Adcock, . .	1727	M.L.	173
„ Susannah and James Aickin, . . .	1738	M.L.	181
Jolly, Thomas and Anne Warren, widow, . .	1735	M.L.	16
Jones, Arthur Oxdstri and Mary Harmon, . .	1675	M.L.	16
„ Catherine and Paul Owrry, . . .	1772	M.L.	8
„ Elinor (widow) and Thomas Young, . .	1729	M.L.	6
„ Elizabeth and Laceshot Dowdall, . .	1715	M.L.	8

CORRECTIONS, DUBLIN GRANT INDEX, 1272–1800—*continued*.

Name, Place, and Occupation.	Year.	Nature of Record.	Page.
Jones, Frances and John Browne,	1137	M.L.	149
„ Francis and Margaret Uggins,	1708	M.L.	163
„ Jane and James Horne,	1680	M.L.	61
„ Robert and Mary Byron,	1737	M.L.	162
„ Robert and Anne Spencer Gibson,	1723	M.L.	11
„ Sarah and William Annesley,	1729	M.L.	69
Jowlan, Deborah and Charles Hamilton,	1731	M.L.	113
Joyce, Susannah and David Fonbally,	1738	M.L.	6
Juge, Isabella and George Willings,	1738	M.L.	63
Julian, George and Margaret Langharne,	1735	M.L.	96
Kade, George and Hannah Bunbury, widow,	1677	M.L.	24
Kaine, Anne (widow) and Richard Mountaigne,	1673	M.L.	17
Karnes, Alice and George Wakefield,	1673	M.L.	61
Katherne, Joseph and Anne Barket, widow,	1671	M.L.	6
Katherine, Thomas and Frances Tyrdell,	1722	M.L.	6
Kan, Mary and John Robinson,	1683	M.L.	61
Kaynan, Agnes and Elizabeth Mountford,	1671	M.L.	3
„ Peter and Elizabeth Tallon,	1728	M.L.	127
Kearns, William and Catherine Banford,	1740	M.L.	73
Keating, John and Mary Filloran,	1734	M.L.	67
Keehan, Margaret and Nicholas Coyle,	1739	M.L.	65
Keom, Mary and Turnan Rocke,	1738	M.L.	70
Keigan, Mary and George Tozpitt,	1673	M.L.	67
Kellinghason, Anne and Rev. Oliam Moller,	1728	M.L.	126
Kelly, Peter and Joan Ellis,	1713	M.L.	3
„ Sarah and William Pane,	1728	M.L.	66
Kelso, John and Susannah Bolland,	1738	M.L.	23
Keanedy, Mariton Janice and Margaret Greagh,	1731	M.L.	153
Keanier, Joshua and Elizabeth Corrill,	1739	M.L.	20
Kenny, Elizabeth and John Gonddison,	1726	M.L.	35
Kernad (or Kermond), Mary (widow) and John Quaie,	1675	M.L.	13
Kerr, Hugh and Esther Fairago,	1728	M.L.	309
Kerres, Jervice and Catherine Whittle,	1731	M.L.	113
Ketamarks, Peter and Elizabeth Thompson,	1677	M.L.	30
Kish, Patrick and Elinor Brice,	1671	M.L.	7
Kieran, Anne and Gerald Grace,	1678	M.L.	30
Kilshew, Thomas and Dorothy Pitta,	1673	M.L.	3

CORRECTIONS, DUBLIN GRANT INDEX, 1272–1800— *continued.*

Name, Place, and Occupation.	Year.	Nature of Record.	Page.
Kinder, Hugh and Isabella Rogers, ...	1672	M.L.	3
King, Dorothy and John Droly, ...	1729	M.L.	10
Kingsmill, Henry and Mary Flood, ...	1702	M.L.	27
Kinkead, Henry and Elizabeth Garnett, . . .	1739	M.L.	24
Kitchen, Jane and Samuel Page, ...	1718	M.L.	30
Knight, Thomas and Rebecca Storm, . . .	1713	M.L.	12
Laban, William and Elizabeth Pells, . . .	1711	M.L.	129
La Bourne, James and Anne Drapier, . .	1723	M.L.	6
La Oasx, Edward and Arabella Vicars, . . .	1760	M.L.	101
Leeboy, Sarah and Benjamin Winterbotham, .	1702	M.L.	179
Lamb, John and Anne Gillard, ...	1729	M.L.	11
Lambert, Robert and Lydia Robinson, widow, .	1730	M.L.	101
Lamane, Mary and John Marlands, . . .	1740	M.L.	105
Land, Hannah and Primrose Maxwell, . . .	1735	M.L.	74
Landers, Joseph and Anne Prentor, . .	1723	M.L.	108
Lane, James and Sarah Adams, . . .	1723	M.L.	12
Langham, Edward and Catherine Brereton, . .	1715	M.L.	17
,, Joseph and Anne Clackson, widow, .	1690	M.L.	61
Langley, John and Elizabeth Stakes, . .	1722	M.L.	8
Langua, Catharine and Henry Corry, . .	1741	M.L.	101
Lapslee, Peter and Elinor Mills, . .	1728	M.L.	108
Lapem, Margaret and Robert Owens, . .	1715	M.L.	8
Latham, Elizabeth and George Hill, . .	1723	M.L.	4
Lathes, Mary and John Mason, . . .	1731	M.L.	102
Lattimore, William and Alice Mason, . .	1731	M.L.	108
Laugharne, Margaret and George Julian, . .	1736	M.L.	3
Laugie, Anne (widow) and Edward Russell, .	1702	M.L.	71
Lauryson, Elizabeth (widow) and Thomas Ewer,	1674	M.L.	11
La Vigne, Mary Anne and James Hoviah, . .	1711	M.L.	105
Lavishire, Anne (widow) and Bernard Morris, .	1731	M.L.	109
Lawrence, Henry and Anne Whitely, . .	1709	M.L.	5
Lawler, Bridget and Peter Courshy, . .	1723	M.L.	101
Lawrence, Laurence and Anne Lewis, . .	1700	M.L.	10
Leaf, John and Susan Whiting, . .	1720	M.L.	105
Leahly, Bridget and Hugh Ware, . .	1739	M.L.	12
Leblanc, Solomon and Jane Dunboig, . .	1715	M.L.	25
Lechford, Mary and Martin Boshell, . .	1715	M.L.	1

CORRECTIONS, DUBLIN GRANT INDEX, 1272–1800—continued.

Name, Place, and Occupation.	Year.	Nature of Record.	Page.
Lea, Anne and William Snail,	1722	M. L.	198
„ Anne and John Whiteing.	1676	M. L.	15
Lemar, John and Eliner Jago,	1739	M.L.	60
Lowe, Elizabeth and John Barker,	1683	M.L.	67
Lethbos, Anne and Philip Emor,	1729	M.L.	50
Le Febure, Catherine and Jonathan Simson,	1733	M.L.	127
Legriner, Martha and William Thompson,	1713	M.L.	188
Lehunt, Jane and George Warburton,	1739	M.L.	69
Leigh, Elizabeth (widow) and Rev. Laurence Neill,	1738	M.L.	20
„ Margaret and William Ousley,	1753	M.L.	6
„ Thomas and Sarah Paris,	1680	M.L.	44
Le Maistrer, Charles and Magdalene Carron (or Curron),	1673	M.L.	3
Le Marchand, Solomon and Eliza Charpless alias Cottnam, widow.	1674	M.L.	11
Leslie, Henry and Amelia Creightonne,	1741	M.L.	109
Lewis, Anne and Laurence Lawrenson,	1720	M.L.	85
„ Joseph and Jane Aubery,	1727	M.L.	179
„ Martha and Denis Haggao,	1737	M.L.	47
Liford, Jane and Thomas Bird,	1674	M.L.	8
Limax, Phylida (widow) and Richard Read,	1709	M.L.	1
Lloyd, Jane and Marro Zackary,	1628	M.L.	63
„ Thos and Joan Price,	1623	M.L.	65
Loach, Eliner and William Ryam,	1714	M.L.	17
Locke, Eliner and Joseph Ashton,	1714	M.L.	19
Lombard, Dominick and Isabella Caldwall,	1673	M.L.	17
Lovelace, Edward and Eliza Blinchaum, widow,	1683	M.L.	71
Lovett, John and Anne Billingsly, widow,	1670	M.L.	45
Low, James and Elizabeth French,	1678	M.L.	85
Lucas, Anne and Christopher Praxey,	1729	M.L.	57
Luther, John and Elizabeth Bowen, widow,	1681	M.L.	44
Lynam, Lotitia (widow) and George Ormerod,	1797	M.L.	43
Lynch, Dominick and Catherine Bourke, widow,	1680	M.L.	44
„ Margaret (widow) and Joseph Aithuson,	1729	M.L.	182
„ Mary and John Houlton,	1730	M.L.	108
„ William and Sibella Blake,	1731	M.L.	132
Lynesius, Mary and Henry Maugh,	1675	M.L.	13
Lyon, Elizabeth and Abraham Jadub,	1710	M.L.	104
„ Mary and Andrew Cronin,	1711	M.L.	131
Lyons, Margaret and John Stephenson,	1731	M.L.	115
„ Mary and James Newton,	1710	M.L.	62

CORRECTIONS, DUBLIN GRANT INDEX, 1272–1800—continued.

Name, Place, and Occupation.	Year.	Nature of Record.	Page
Mabbott, Diana and Sir Henry Tuite, knight, .	1675	M.L.	16
M'Cabe, Eugene and Lepida Simpson, .	1726	M.L.	78
M'Cardy, Samuel and Ann Maradine, .	1729	M.L.	16
M'Causland, John and Anne Sampson, .	1718	M.L.	57
M'Clarie, Jane and Henry Bunbury, .	1724	M.L.	77
M'Ginne, Mary and John Curtlies, .	1713	M.L.	4
M'Gilliser, Elinor and Samuel Goodbody, .	1725	M.L.	101
M'Gennell, John and Elizabeth Fider, .	1761	M.L.	15
M'Cright, Elizabeth (widow) and William Davison, .	1733	M.L.	31
M'Cullugh, John and Grace Percivall, .	1727	M.L.	31
M'Daniel, (——) (widow) and John King, .	1579	M.L.	3
M'Donnagh, William and Catherine Shanervare, .	1737	M.L.	149
M'Gill, John (Sir, Bart.), and Lady Arabella Susan Hamilton,	1663	M.L.	6
M'Gusty, David and Frances Goodwin, .	1731	M.L.	115
Mack, Anne and Henry Davis .	1729	M.L.	4
Ewch and Jane Pearie, .	1729	M.L.	70
M'Kittrick, Catherine and John Ditchfield, .	1766	M.L.	8
M'Mahon, Patrick and Bridget Fierash, .	1759	M.L.	17
M'Maughan, James and Mary Butler, .	1727	M.L.	8
M'Mullen, Anne and Joseph Castlin, .	1761	M.L.	127
M'Murran, Henry and Mary Smith, .	1733	M.L.	8
M'Neal, Elizabeth and John Chambers, .	1748	M.L.	8
M'Neale, Mary (widow) and John Fraley, .	1730	M.L.	8
M'Quaid, Margaret and Patrick Corrigan, .	1711	M.L.	128
M'Waitle, Jane and James Jackson, .	1728	M.L.	125
Maddock, Ann and Lewis Bonnoin, .	1768	M.L.	3
Maffett, William and Elizabeth Carrak, .	1734	M.L.	14
Magrath, James and Margaret Scratch, .	1738	M.L.	125
Malody, Mary and Thomas Peele, .	1654	M.L.	11
Mangan, Catherine and Thomas Cork, .	1731	M.L.	108
Mann, Mary (widow) and William Chabener, .	1680	M.L.	110
Mary and William Sempill, .	1700	M.L.	13
Marmun, Moses and Mary Garnett, .	1653	M.L.	15
Markefield, William and Susannah Grace, .	1728	M.L.	13
Marlande, John and Mary Lamena, .	1760	M.L.	100
Marples, Mary and Francis Snicke, .	1711	M.L.	11
Marrott, Mary (widow) and Ralph Card, .	1717	M.L.	13
Martin, James and Edith Finneran, .	1754	M.L.	6
Martin, Clement and Margaret Saddleton, .	1676	M.L.	30

CORRECTIONS, DUBLIN GRANT INDEX, 1372-1800—*continued*.

Name, Place, and Occupation.	Year.	Nature of Record.	Page.
Martin, Elizabeth and William Phillips,	1740	M.L.	63
„ John and Mary Fekes,	1737	M.L.	174
Maredine, Ann and Samuel M'Cardy,	1709	M.L.	65
Mason, John and Mary Lalben,	1738	M.L.	312
„ Thomas and Elizabeth Albritain, widow,	1737	M.L.	163
Massey, Edss and James Hardswick,	1728	M.L.	38
„ Huxb and Emy Beawon,	1681	M.L.	18
Mason, Pierre and Mary Mould, widow,	1679	M.L.	38
Masset, Alice and William Lattimore,	1731	M.L.	188
Masters, John and Jane Yeates,	1681	M.L.	64
Mather, Anne (widow) and Joseph Scott,	1673	M.L.	6
Mathers, Mary (widow) and Charles Empson,	1673	M.L.	4
Mathews, Hester and William Mosely,	1682	M.L.	64
Mathews, Hannah (widow) and James Robertson,	1737	M.L.	66
Maudly, Elizabeth and John Standly,	1740	M.L.	63
Maudsley, Christopher and Elizabeth Raymond,	1723	M.L.	26
Maxzen, John and Mary Holt,	1728	M.L.	163
Maxwell, Primrose and Hannah Land,	1726	M.L.	71
May, Daniel and Bridget Greener,	1717	M.L.	29
„ Walter and Mary Jacob,	1673	M.L.	5
Mead, Benjamin and Elizabeth Bowrie,	1684	M.L.	77
Mealnes, Christopher and Ursula Andrews, widow,	1672	M.L.	33
Mealer, Mary and James Cummins,	1708	M.L.	181
Menthard, Charles and Sarah Verbrun,	1763	M.L.	82
Meluen, Thomas and Isabella Sibson,	1734	M.L.	64
Meenan, Margaret and Daniel Crosbie,	1737	M.L.	189
Meleap, Jane (widow) and Samuel Bowdon,	1675	M.L.	14
Madlicott, Elizabeth and Hugh Hoghs,	1739	M.L.	86
Meffitt, Francis and Elizabeth Corran,	1741	M.L.	111
Meley, Mary and Robert Clouch,	1673	M.L.	3
Mendy, William and Hester Mathewes,	1683	M.L.	64
Mercier, Charles and Hester Dupuy,	1714	M.L.	21
Meredith, Charles and Judith Savage,	1677	M.L.	25
„ Edward and Elizabeth Chandler, widow,	1684	M.L.	77
„ William and Mary Armstrong, widow,	1733	M.L.	20
Merridith, Thomas and Catherine Duros,	1734	M.L.	197
Meverell, Sarah and Daniel Oakey,	1673	M.L.	9
Middleton, Mary and Manuel Oonin,	1711	M.L.	11
Mills, Andrew and Sarah Hill,	1739	M.L.	166

CORRECTIONS, DUBLIN GRANT INDEX, 1273-1800—*continued.*

Name, Place, and Occupation.	Year.	Nature of Record.	Page.
Mills, Elinor and Peter Lapaine,	1728	M.L.	105
„ James and Mary Hale,	1709	M.L.	113
„ Sarah and Thomas Williams,	1790	M.L.	44
Minnitt, Margaret and John Hartley,	1737	M.L.	173
Mitchel, Frances and William Wills,	1728	M.L.	31
Mitchell, Anne and Thomas Bewley,	1676	M.L.	16
„ Mary and John Kelln,	1725	M.L.	60
Mogan, Ann and John Fetherston,	1711	M.L.	129
Molineux, William and Lucy Domvill,	1678	M.L.	6
Mollos, Antoinette and Bernard Villeneufve,	1714	M L.	2
Mollineux, Robert and Mary Stodart,	1683	M.L.	71
Montgomery, Catherine (Lady) and Francis Hamilton,	1676	M.L.	2
Moor, Catherine and Patrick Gallan,	1718	M.L.	1
Moore, Elizabeth and William Nanfan,	1705	M.L.	9
„ Elizabeth and Frand Tydd,	1725	M.L.	133
„ Pierce and Catherine Dovey,	1711	M.L.	118
Moorhead, Martha and William Nelson,	1729	M.L.	90
Morand, Francis and Mary Elizabeth Charcarier, widow,	1743	M.L.	173
Moran, Mary and Peter Gembel,	1714	M.L.	7
Morgan, Charles and Elinor Humphrie, widow,	1733	M.L.	9
„ (George) and Elizabeth Eaton, widow,	1716	M.L.	9
„ Susannah (widow) and William Creech,	1741	M.L.	60
Murphy, Anne (widow) and Richard Dowdall,	1728	M.L.	161
Morris, Bernard and Anne Lavishire, widow,	1731	M.L.	179
„ June and Benjamin Crumley,	1733	M.L.	9
„ John and Jane Nicholson, widow,	1677	M.L.	9
„ Katherine and Robert Casey,	1728	M.L.	63
Morton, Margaret and Robert Parry,	1729	M.L.	9a
„ Mary (widow) and John Stanly,	1676	M.L.	9
„ Sarah and Peter Butche,	1679	M.L.	1
Mos, Alls and James Brealy,	1683	M.L.	9
Moss, Judith and Daniel Oakey,	1680	M.L.	9
Motley, Mary (widow) and William Ellis,	1728	M.L.	57
Mould, Mary (widow) and Pierre Masson,	1679	M L.	74
Moulsworth, Robert and Letitia Coote,	1676	M L.	21
Mornelsw, Jane (widow) and Humphry Barnes,	1719	M.L.	8
Mount, Tabitha (widow) and Sir John Tolly,	1678	M.L.	9
Mountinge, Richard and Anne Kahoe, widow,	1676	M L.	13
Mountford, Elizabeth and James Kearnas,	1676	M.L.	9

CORRECTIONS, DUBLIN GRANT INDEX, 1272–1800—continued.

Name, Place, and Occupation.	Year.	Nature of Record.	Page.
Mason, John and Mary Parsons, widow.	1073	M L.	25
Moyett, John and Mary Taylor.	1641	M.L.	71
Mulcaill, William and Mary Byrne.	1749	M L.	65
Mullody, Anthony and Jane Worship.	1675	M.L.	13
Munns, William and Dorothy Story.	1631	M.L.	59
Murphy, Elinor and Charles Alder.	1738	M.L.	103
,, Thomas and Rose Booth.	1679	M.L.	2
Murry, John and Mary Lynch, widow.	1740	M.L.	70
Mushett, Rev. William and Anne Smyth.	1749	M.L.	105
Musson, William (junior) and Margaret Denby.	1737	M L.	104
Mathum, Martha and John Read.	7731	M.L.	121
Muty, Anne and Benjamin Constable.	1737	M.L.	49
Myers, William and Mary Hartington.	1677	M.L.	21
Nelly, John and Sarah Carter.	1711	M.L.	112
Nanton, William and Elizabeth Moore.	1724	M.L.	36
Nash, Mary (widow) and Joseph Osbyrne.	1728	M.L.	61
,, Maurice and Mary Botsford.	1725	M L.	26
Nelms, Anthony (or Holme) and Rebecca Swift, widow.	1620	M.L.	49
Nelson, William and Martha Moorhead.	1778	M.L.	709
Nevett, Caleb and Thomasan Eckersly.	1739	M.L.	90
New, William and Mary Bignall.	1714	M.L.	16
Newcome, Catherine (widow) and William Cuthbert.	1674	M.L.	10
Newotmen, Charles and Charlotte Behe.	1746	M.L.	89
Newgint, Lewalin and Catharine Royce alias Ferrely, widow.	1729	M.L.	129
Newton, James and Mary Lyons.	1729	M L.	93
Nicholson, Jane (widow) and John Morris.	1677	M.L.	89
Nimme, Elizabeth and George Charters.	1746	M.L.	63
Nix, Stephen and Winifred Ashley.	1715	M.L.	72
Nixon, Mary and James Taylor.	1710	M.L.	108
Norcott, John and Mary Irwyn.	1732	M.L.	89
Norris, Mary and Francis Hazlen.	1715	M.L.	21
Norton, Samuel and Frances Aigula.	1729	M.L.	67
Nowland, Lydia and George Blake.	1733	M.L.	15
Noy, Barbara and William Green.	1739	M.L.	63
Nugent, Mary and Charles Barker.	1741	M.L.	111
Nunn, Benjamin and Anne Steel, widow.	1738	M.L.	131
Nuttall, Charles and Anne Britton.	1738	M.L.	134
Nyler, Elizabeth (widow) and William Swift.	1635	M.L.	10

CORRECTIONS, DUBLIN GRANT INDEX, 1273–1300—*continued*

Name, Place, and Occupation.	Year.	Nature of Record.	Page.
Oakey, Daniel and Sarah Meverell, . . .	1679	M.L.	1
„ Daniel and Judith Moss, . . .	1680	M.L.	9
O'Brien, Donal and —— Gray, widow, .	1677	M.L.	7
O'Hara, Dorothy and James Smith, .	1710	M.L.	8
Oldfield, Anne and Cornelius Quignan, .	1690	M.L.	9
O'Neale, Elizabeth and Thomas Pearce, .	1732	M.L.	54
Ord, Thomas and Jane Clark, . . .	1725	M.L.	3
„ Thomas and Mary Lawson, widow, .	1729	M.L.	3
Ormerod, George and Letitia Lymam, . .	1737	M.L.	6
„ Mary (widow) and Edward Green, .	1727	M.L.	15
Ormond, James and Elizabeth (Earl and Countess of), Licence to eat meat during Lent.	1679	--	3
Ormsby, William and Catherine Graydon, . .	1733	M.L.	76
Osbyrne, Joseph and Mary Nash, widow, .	1728	M.L.	8
Ottiwell, Henry and Susannah Fisher, . .	1733	M.L.	71
Oulton, Walter and Lucy Prosser, . .	1731	M.L.	18
Oasley, William and Margaret Leigh, . .	1733	M.L.	9
Owens, Robert and Margaret Lapur, . .	1729	M.L.	8
Owin, Anne (widow) and James Potter, .	1691	M.L.	8
Page, Samuel and Jane Kitchen, . .	1725	M.L.	9
Paine, Sarah and William Jenkins, . .	1740	M.L.	52
Palmer, Jeffery and Elizabeth Wetherby, .	1740	M.L.	6
Pana, William and Sarah Kelly, . .	1749	M.L.	64
Parry, Elinor and Owen Hughes, . .	1671	M.L.	8
„ Robert and Margaret Morton, .	1729	M.L.	61
Parsons, Mary (alias Cosby), widow, and Peter Clinton, .	1674	M.L.	1
Partington, Peter and Mary Storms, widow, .	1683	M.L.	8
Parvain, Susan and Thomas Cumbrell, .	1737	M.L.	8
Jarvinale, Mary (widow) and Henry Grant, . .	1730	M.L.	113
Passmore, Margaret and Samuel Todger, .	1737	M.L.	3
Pattison, Hannah and William Johnson, .	1733	M.L.	7
Pataric, Jane and Enoch Mack, . . .	1735	M.L.	139
Passy, Christopher and Anne Lucas, .	1729	M.L.	5
Payne, Rose (widow) and Philip Bostwick, . .	1720	M.L.	6
Peart, Thomas and Elizabeth O'Neale, . .	1729	M.L.	138
Pearson, Frances (widow) and Henry Bellwood, . .	1741	M.L.	138
Peale, Thomas and Mary Maloody, .	1684	M.L.	74
Perry, Robert and Anne Cooley, . .	1730	M.L.	88
„ Thomas and Elinor Graves, widow, . .	1737	M.L.	107

CORRECTIONS, DUBLIN GRANT INDEX, 1272–1800—*continued.*

Name, Place, and Occupation.	Year.	Nature of Record.	Page.
Pegnal, Margaret and Henry Syuge, . .	1757	M. L.	119
Pails, Elizabeth and William Lehan, .	1711	M. L.	110
Peirs, Grace and Charles Ros, ...	1784	M. L.	89
Palm, Elizabeth and Maurice Boslacy, . . . , .	1683	M. L.	65
Pell, Hannah and Gilbert Plumber, . . . ,	1757	M. L.	43
Pender, Jane and Michael Downey. . . .	1739	M. L.	66
Pennington, Marjery (widow) and John Galleford, . .	1677	M. L.	53
Pennix, George and Elizabeth Gans, . . .	1716	M. L.	164
Perams, Edward and Mary Whemily, widow, .	1686	M. L.	17
Percivall, Edward and Jane Charleton, . .	1711	M. L.	152
„ Grace and John M'Cullagh, . .	1787	M. L.	30
Perrit, Thomas and Mary Ball, ...	1714	M. L.	15
Perry, Elizabeth and John Higgins, . . .	1728	M. L.	158
Peter, Walter and Anne Surdivell, . . .	1675	M. L.	14
Pethin, William and Elizabeth Aubury, . .	1682	M. L.	59
Pettit, Elinor and William Cranton, . . .	1694	M. L.	71
Phillips, William and Elizabeth Martin, . .	1710	M. L.	63
Phillips, Elizabeth and Abraham Rogers, . .	1739	M. L.	60
Phillipson, William and Mary Holcomb, . .	1783	M. L.	181
Phipps, Elizabeth and John Penn, . . .	1729	M. L.	125
Piaknoll, Hugh and Hannah Ballentine, . .	1726	M. L.	76
Piddock, Elizabeth (widow) and John Bourk, . .	1711	M L.	17
Pierson, Ellen and Rev. Thomas Thornton. .	1714	M. L.	14
Piggot, John and Catherine Babbington, widow, .	1710	M. L.	22
Piggott, Judith and Francis Cosby, . . .	1733	M. L.	60
Pike, Elizabeth and John Raper, . . .	1682	M. L.	63
Pilsworth, Ralph and Martha Waller, . .	1711	M. L.	126
Pindar, Richard and Elizabeth Bambrook, . .	1731	M L.	173
Pinnent, Jane and George Scowcraft, . . .	1678	M. L.	10
Pitts, Dorothy and Thomas Kinshaw. . .	1673	M. L.	8
„ Thomas and Frances Allen. . . .	1733	M L.	151
Plowman, Elizabeth (widow) and John Plookes, .	1685	M. L.	79
Plumber, Gilbert and Hannah Pell. . .	1757	M. L.	43
Plumer, Hannah and William Evoy. . .	1687	M. L.	53
Potter, James and Anne Owls, widow, . .	1681	M. L.	67
Powell, William and Elizabeth Stones, . .	1714	M. L.	18
Prandil, Maudlin and John Oswalo, . . .	1735.	M. L.	173
Price, [ ] and [ ] Delange, . . .	1678	M. L.	33
„ Anne and Richard Brumton, . . .	1728	M. L.	184

CORRECTIONS, DUBLIN GRANT INDEX, 1272–1800—*continued*.

Name, Place, and Occupation.	Year.	Nature of Record.	Page.
Price, Dorothy (widow) and John Crampion,	1727	M.L.	58
„ Joan and Thos Lloyd,	1683	M.L.	6
Price, Margaret and John Danson,	1729	M L.	136
Pringle, Lydia (widow) and Archibald Boyle,	1713	M.L.	4
Procter, Mary and Joseph Shaw,	1690	M.L.	9
Proctor, Anne and Joseph Langley,	1728	M.L.	129
Proteau, Lucy and Walley Oulton,	1731	M.L.	116
Pullin, Mary and Nicholas Hatch,	1672	M.L.	24
Purcer, William and Anne Reilly, widow,	1777	M.L.	37
Quale, John and Mary Kermud, widow,	1676	M.L.	11
Quaterman, Matthew and Dorothy Dooly,	1676	M.L.	16
Quesqui, Mary Louise (de Challais) and Rev. Marie Anthony Krebourbale Vinoheo Des Voeux,	1735	M L.	17
Question, Anne and Joseph Badcock,	1714	M.L.	16
Quin, Anne and Thomas Lynch,	1711	M.L.	119
„ Hector and John Carbey,	1686	M.L.	6
Quinan, Mary (or Quinne) and John Butler,	1673	M.L.	4
Quinn, Edmund and Jane Eaton,	1676	M.L.	14
Quinlan, Cornelius and Anne Oldfield,	1680	M.L.	6
Quoulan, Elizabeth (widow) and John Rea,	1683	M.L.	6
Radford, Nathaniel and Frances Boyes,	1730	M.L.	116
Raines, Elizabeth (widow) and Charles Butler,	1713	M.L.	4
Raives, Mary (widow) and William Carpenter,	1711	M.L.	16
Rapee, John and Elizabeth Pike,	1681	M.L.	6
Rasby, Christopher and Martha Watchman,	1691	M.L.	11
Rathbone, William and Sarah Greenwood, widow,	1789	M.L.	189
Ratliffe, Anne and Henry Richardson,	1740	M.L.	16
Raymond, Elizabeth and Christopher Mandsley,	1723	M.L.	31
Rea, John and Elizabeth Quoniam, widow,	1683	M.L.	6
Read, John and Martha Matham,	1781	M.L.	16
„ Richard and Phyllis Linnar, widow,	1726	M.L.	4
Reaumes, Rachel and Peter Cross,	1786	M.L.	44
Reboul, Peter Cousins and Antoinette Barejore,	1729	M.L.	12
„ Rachel and Cæsar Combe,	1787	M L.	6
(Rescault), or Rascauly.			
Reed, Anne and Andrew Cunningham,	1723	M.L.	3

CORRECTIONS, DUBLIN GRANT INDEX, 1272–1800—*continued.*

Name, Place, and Occupation.	Year.	Nature of Record.	Page.
Reed, Charles and Tabitha Cadwallader,	1729	M.L.	64
„ Michael and Catherine Wheelwright,	1714	M.L.	13
Reeve, Joseph and Frances Hatcher, widow,	1677	M.L.	29
Regnant, Hannah and Boyle Bagwell,	1728	M.L.	62
Reilly, Ann (widow) and William Purcer,	1787	M.L.	37
„ Christopher and Mary Hamilton,	1722	M.L.	63
Relick, William and Sarah Hanlon,	1692	M.L.	61
Rollink, Mary (widow) and John Healy,	1685	M.L.	78
Rencesely, Paul (Recoulet) and Rachel Dagoe,	1793	M.L.	18
Reynolds, Catherine and Christopher Britt,	1735	M.L.	77
Rhodes, Mary and Nicholas Sator,	1713	M.L.	3
Rialton, Andrew and Elinor Brazill, widow,	1722	M.L.	129
Rice, Susannah (widow) and Augustin Ivers,	1714	M.L.	38
Richardson, Henry and Anne Ratliffe,	1729	M.L.	66
„ Hugh and Anne Lamb,	1730	M.L.	93
„ Thomas and Nicla Sisephena,	1677	M.L.	24
Rickinson, John and Catherine Walsh,	1728	M.L.	63
Richyson, James and Priscilla Gwither,	1734	M.L.	44
Rigby, Alexander and Mary Brunswich, widow,	1682	M.L.	59
Right, Alice and Charles Tindall,	1673	M.L.	13
Riley, Edward and Mary Horton,	1678	M.L.	15
Rippingham, Edmond and Easter Desmyators,	1740	M.L.	94
Ritchasson, Eliza (widow) and Edward Lovelace,	1682	M.L.	71
Robertson, James and Hannah Mathews, widow,	1787	M.L.	43
Robinson, Isaac and John Ingham,	1729	M.L.	62
„ John and Mary Kitt,	1683	M.L.	69
„ Lydia (widow) and Robert Lambart,	1739	M.L.	101
„ Mary (widow) and Edward Swettenham,	1729	M.L.	71
Robison, Sarah and William Dunn,	1711	M.L.	131
Rokoka, Richard, Cokyston, Tallaght,	1556	O.W.	—
Rocke, Anne and Gaspard Tellier,	1725	M.L.	51
Roe, Mary and James Threshold,	1731	M.L.	117
Rogers, Abraham and Elizabeth Philips,	1739	M.L.	62
„ Jane and James Dawson,	1678	M.L.	18
„ Thomas and Isabella Blansfield, widow,	1734	M.L.	65
Rome, Comfort and John Barber,	1730	M.L.	107 & 110
Rooth, Rose and Thomas Murphy,	1678	M.L.	8
Roper, Samuel and Sarah Sunderland,	1727	M.L.	148
Rorke, Turtan and Mary Keene,	1729	M.L.	70

CORRECTIONS, DUBLIN GRANT INDEX, 1272-1800—*continued.*

No.	Name, Place, and Occupation.	Year.	Nature of Record.	Page.
	Ross, George and Elinor Driskall, . . .	1723	M.L.	69
	Ross, Marjory and James Simpson, . . .	1731	M.L.	70
	Rossell, Thomas and Sarah Wolfenden, . . .	1730	M.L.	8
	Roiton, John and Bridget Stearns, . . .	1677	M.L.	8
	Rougier, Peter and Anne Guinet, . . .	1735	M.L.	6
	Roulila, John and Frances Howrall, . . .	1714	M.L.	13
	Row, Mary and Francis Stow, . . .	1714	M.L.	11
	Rowlandson, Elizabeth and Samuel Walton, . .	1673	M.L.	1
	Rowlett, John and Anne Wills, . . .	1734	M.L.	10
	Rowley, Thomas and Anne Mitchell, . . .	1675	M.L.	14
	Royne, Catharine (alias Pericly), widow, and Lawelin Newgint.	1735	M.L.	111
	Rulland, Mary and Mathurin Ardouin, . .	1730	M.L.	9
	Russell, Edward and Anne Langia, widow. . .	1729	M.L.	7
	„ Philip, St. Nicholas Within, Dublin, . .	28 Hen. VI.	W.	Plea R. 62
	Rutledge, Anne (widow) and John Swann. . .	1676	M.L.	9
	Butler, Joseph and Eliza Brimmerade. . .	1676	M.L.	8
	„ Rachel and Sherm Cove, . . .	1677	M.L.	6
	Rylan, Anne (widow) and John Stone, . . .	1680	M.L.	10
	St. Vast, Tannerguy and Jane Bery, . . .	1673	M.L.	27
	Sall, William and Anne Lea, . . .	1729	M.L.	89
	Sampson, Anne and John M'Cansland, . . .	1708	M.L.	9
	„ Mary Ann and James Echlin, . . .	1709	M.L.	9
	„ Robert and Letitia Forward, . . .	1725	M.L.	9
	Sanders, Anthony and Phœbe Scatney, . .	1701	M.L.	102
	Sanderton, Margaret and Clement Martin, . .	1678	M.L.	30
	Savage, Judith and Charles Meredith, . .	1677	M.L.	75
	Scarlet, Anne and Richard White, . . .	1671	M.L.	7
	Scarnfield, Anne and Philip Weeks, . . .	1725	M.L.	155
	Scatney, Phœbe and Anthony Sanders, . .	1701	M.L.	113
	Scott, Anne and James Wall, . . .	1731	M.L.	121
	„ John and Elizabeth Ellers, . . .	1734	M.L.	10
	„ Joseph and Anne Mather, widow, . .	1678	M.L.	1
	Scoverah, George and Joan Pimmen, . .	1676	M.L.	9
	Scratt, Samuel (Rev.) and Hester Walker, widow, . .	1657	M.L.	30
	Scayle, Elizabeth and Josiah Jackson, . .	1734	M.L.	9
	Seawell, Hester and James Heire or Haige, . .	1683	M.L.	9

CORRECTIONS, DUBLIN GRANT INDEX, 1272-1800—*continued.*

Name, Place, and Occupation.	Year.	Nature of Record.	Page.
Semple, William and Mary Mann,	1740	M.L.	72
Sergia, Felician and Frances Hugginson,	1790	M.L.	108
Sharman, Christopher and Mary Durall, widow,	1738	M.L.	815
Sharman, Margaret (widow) and Thomas Hammond,	1725	M.L.	22
Mary, Daniel and Catherine Derman,	1731	M.L.	118
Sharpe, Honor and Philip Tuit,	1678	M.L.	13
Shaughnessy, Catherine and William M'Donnagh,	1737	M.L.	159
Sheridan, Diana (widow) and Henry Byrne,	1710	M.L.	68
Sherrer, Richard and Jane Descombe,	1723	M.L.	34
Shaw, Anne and William Hughs,	1729	M.L.	74
Shinlal, Anne and Benjamin Tattersen,	1738	M.L.	84
Shippabottom, Judith and Richard Addy,	1738	M.L.	504
Shirlow, Henry and Anne Armestronge,	1672	M.L.	8
Short, Elizabeth and Richard Ward,	1674	M.L.	7
Sibson, Elizabeth and Allen Barker,	1673	M.L.	88
— Isabella and Thomas Mecham,	1734	M.L.	48
Sillard, Anne and John Lamb,	1710	M.L.	11
Simpson, James and Marjory Rosse,	1732	M.L.	178
— Lepida and Eugene M'Cabe,	1735	M.L.	79
— Margaret (widow) and Thomas Timperoe,	1673	M.L.	18
Simson, Sarah and Mark Grimwood,	1737	M.L.	36
Skelven, Elizabeth and Vincent Dobson,	1679	M.L.	60
Slattis, Catherine and Francis Farrel,	1738	M.L.	199
Slyng, Mary and John Allinson,	1731	M.L.	116
Smuly, Sarah and Andrew Dunlop,	1725	M.L.	28
Smart, Joseph and Sarah Chadhorne,	1725	M.L.	23
— Mary (widow) and John Smith,	1673	M.L.	4
Smith, Anne and John Allen,	1708	M.L.	9
— Barbara (widow) and Thomas Atkin,	1679	M.L.	43
— Elinor and Arthur Walker,	1742	M.L.	180
— Isabella and James Watson,	1711	M.L.	119
— James and Dorothy O'Hara,	1710	M.L.	88
— Jane and Richard Bourne,	1708	M.L.	118
— John (junior) and Jane Harman,	1708	M.L.	59
— Margaret and Andrew Golding,	1708	M.L.	71
— Mary and Rev. Thomas Aston,	1678	M.L.	31
— Mary and Henry M'Murren,	1728	M.L.	13
— Nathan and Priscilla Oakhmen,	1731	M.L.	56
Smoke, Francis and Mary Marples,	1711	M.L.	11

CORRECTIONS, DUBLIN GRANT INDEX, 1272-1800 --continued.

Name, Place, and Occupation.	Year.	Nature of Record.	Page.
Smith, John and Mary Stuart, widow,	1673	M.L.	1
Southwell, Thomas George (Hon.) and Margaret Cecil Hamilton.	1741	M.L.	18
Spence, James and Jane Why,	1653	M.L.	71
Spring, Sibella and John Humfrey,	1739	M.L.	18
Squire, Susan and George Dodson.	1738	M.L.	80
Stafford, Thomas and Susannah Vanhorn.	1741	M.L.	18
Stakes, Elizabeth and John Langley,	1733	M.L.	4
„ Nathaniel and Anne Wade,	1733	M.L.	12
„ Susannah and John Constable,	1730	M.L.	60
Scraddy, John and Elizabeth Manlly,	1769	M.L.	18
Stanly, John and Mary Morton, widow.	1676	M.L.	60
Stearns, Bridget and John Roston,	1687	M.L.	9
Steel, Anne (widow) and Benjamin Nunn.	1722	M.L.	12
„ Elinor and Michael Browne,	1737	M.L.	14
„ Rachel and James Trimble,	1728	M.L.	13
Steels, Laurence and Sarah Fernley,	1738	M.L.	60
Stephens, Ninia and Thomas Richardson.	1677	M.L.	24
Stephens, Alice and Thomas Boll,	1684	M.L.	14
Stephenson, John and Margaret Lyons,	1731	M.L.	18
Sterne, Mary (widow) and Peter Parthurton,	1822	M.L.	8
Stewart, Ephraim and Susannah Wills,	1731	M.L.	8
Suldaum, Elizabeth and Gilbert Hutchinson,	1678	M.L.	24
Stiles, William and Catherine Toy,	1715	M.L.	0
Stocks, Elizabeth and Thomas Flood,	1633	M.L.	6
Stodart, Mary and Robert Molliness,	1683	M.L.	71
Stogdill, John and Sarah Williams,	1710	M.L.	6
Stone, John and Anne Bryden, widow,	1635	M.L.	8
Stonem, Elizabeth and William Powell,	1714	M.L.	12
„ Jane (widow) and Francis Style,	1631	M.L.	74
Story, Dorothy and William Munns,	1633	M.L.	8
„ Elizabeth (widow) and John Chatwell,	17.0	M.L.	4
„ Elizabeth and Jervis Fox,	17.3	M.L.	12
Stow, Francis and Mary Row,	1711	M.L.	11
Stradloth, Oloanna and Carlo Tamburn,	1729	M.L.	41
Straughan, Alexander and Jane Turner, widow,	1746	M.L.	6
Straw, Joseph and Mary Procter,	1660	M.L.	0
Stretch, Margaret and James Magrath,	1735	M.L.	18
Strong, Bridget and Joseph Broonly,	1729	M.L.	80
Sturgeon, George and Jane Dowglass,	1714	M.L.	6

CORRECTIONS, DUBLIN GRANT INDEX, 1272–1800—*continued.*

Name, Place and Occupation.	Year.	Nature of Record.	Page.
Styd, Francis and Jane Flomes, widow,	1634	M.L.	70
Sullivan, Elizabeth (widow) and Thomas Grant,	1788	M.L.	61
Sunderland, Sarah and Samuel Roper,	1787	M.L.	168
Sardivall, Anne and Walter Puter.	1676	M.L.	11
Suter, Nicholas and Mary Rhodes,	1713	M.L.	3
Satton, Catherine and James Dixon,	1631	M.L.	35
Swan, Bellingham (Rev.) and Martha Aikin,	1730	M.L.	30
„ William and Frances Horish,	1740	M.L.	109
Swann, John and Anne Rutledge, widow,	1678	M.L.	18
Swords, John and Elizabeth Archer,	1714	M.L.	10
Swetenham, Edward and Mary Robinson, widow,	1733	M.L.	71
Swift, Rebecca (widow), and Anthony Holme or Nolms,	1680	M.L.	48
„ William and Dorothy Barretone, widow,	1574	M.L.	6
„ William and Elizabeth Nyler, widow,	1633	M.L.	80
Swinfield, Susan and John Grevell,	1631	M.L.	57
Syles, Thomas (or Styles) and Deborah Thompson,	1679	M.L.	31
Symons, Elizabeth and Humphrey Burre,	1661	M.L.	73
Syage, Henry and Margaret Prynel,	1737	M.L.	171
Tachard, Elizabeth (widow) and John Vabres,	1719	M.L.	57
Tadpole, Anne and Joachim Falconberge,	1683	M.L.	62
Talloe, Elizabeth and Peter Kearnan,	1738	M.L.	137
„ John and Delphina Bird,	1744	M.L.	122
Tambara, Carlo and Giosama Stradioth,	1725	M.L.	41
Tanner, Paul and Mary Cengl,	1722	M.L.	133
Tasker, John and Sarah Cane,	1673	M.L.	17
„ Mary and Thomas Wilkinson,	1651	M.L.	61
Tatham, John and Mary Torlington, widow,	1676	M.L.	73
Tetteroen, Benjamin and Anne Shiplnt,	1780	M.L.	34
Taylor, George and Mary Cavard,	1631	M.L.	51
„ James and Sarah Gibell,	1753	M.L.	113
„ James and Mary Niana,	1710	M.L.	103
„ Joseph and Abigail Ferreare,	1729	M.L.	73
„ Mary and John Moyeth,	1684	M.L.	76
Tee, Barnaby and Cicily Grumly,	1710	M.L.	73
Talliser, Gaspard and Anne Rocke,	1733	M.L.	31
Templeton, James and Anne Whitney. widow,	1733	M.L.	11

CORRECTIONS, DUBLIN GRANT INDEX, 1272-1800—*continued.*

Name, Place, and Occupation.	Year.	Nature of Record.	Page.
Tomlson, John and Anne Bolton, ...	1713	M.L.	1
Toppins, George and Mary Keigan. . . .	1673	M.L.	2
Thornton, Mary and James Brerely. . . .	1680	M.L.	611
Thomlinson, Elizabeth and James Butler. . .	1780	M.L.	181
Thompson, Elizabeth and Peter Ketemarks. . .	1677	M.L.	3
" Martha and William Vanderhagan. .	1730	M.L.	100
" Mary and John Crosby, . . .	1730	M.L.	114
" William and Martha Legalner, .	1730	M.L.	118
Threlkald, James and Mary Roe. . . .	1781	M.L.	117
Thwaites, Ann and Nathaniel Weld, . . .	1741	M.L.	116
Timperon, Thomas and Margaret Simpson, widow, .	1676	M.L.	11
Tindall, Charles and Allen Right. . . .	1675	M.L.	12
Tobin, Abraham and Elizabeth Baker. . .	1736	M.L.	117
Totty, John (Sir) and Tabitha Monnt, widow. .	1673	M.L.	13
Touler, Rose and George Fisher. . . .	1731	M.L.	16
Travers, Hannah (widow) and John Helms. . .	1711	M.L.	19
Tremble, Nathaniel and Catherine Chapman. .	1681	M.L.	34
Trench, Elizabeth and George Warburton. . .	1735	M.L.	138
" Judith and Samuel Coock. . .	1735	M.L.	8
" Mary and William Vaughan. . .	1730	M.L.	90
Trim, George and Elizabeth Harrison. . .	1737	M.L.	143
Trinkle, James and Rachel Steel. . . .	1721	M.L.	124
Trinkey, Margaret and John Tile. . . .	1731	M.L.	119
Truffitt, Jane and Richard Castle. . . .	1739	M.L.	8
Trulye, John and Susannah Bryer. . . .	1726	M.L.	18
Tralyer, Percife Mary and Simon Boulgne. . .	1730	M.L.	16
Tryddle, William (Rev.) and Anne Dobson. . .	1737	M.L.	147
Trydell, Frances and Thomas Katherine. . .	1738	M.L.	6
Tait, Philip and Honor Sharpe	1670	M.L.	9
Tuite, Sir Henry (knight) and Diana Mablott. .	1675	M.L.	11
Turner, Jane (widow) and Alexander Straughan. .	1770	M.L.	12
" Thomas and Mary Hatton. . .	1737	M.L.	148
Turnly, Mary and John Cadis, ...	1711	M.L.	13
Tastian, William and Martha Bill. . . .	1681	M.L.	11
Tydd, Frend and Elizabeth Moore. . . .	1735	M.L.	133
Tygart, Mary (widow) and John Darragh. . .	1780	M.L.	161
Tyler, John and Elizabeth Hankleon. . . .	1709	M.L.	6
Tyrer, Elizabeth and Nathaniel Weld. . . .	1683	M.L.	6

CORRECTIONS, DUBLIN GRANT INDEX, 1272-1800—continued.

Name, Place, and Occupation.	Year.	Nature of Record.	Page.
Uniack, Richard and Eliza Hackdailor, . . .	1680	M.L.	18
Springhams, Dorothy (widow) and Christopher Hulgan,	1621	M.L.	79
Vakres, John and Elizabeth Tachard, widow, . .	1718	M.L.	87
Vanderhagan, William and Martha Thompson, . .	1789	M.L.	149
Venhara, Susannah and Thomas Stafford, . . .	1741	M.L.	112
Van Kruys Kirchen, Heyndrich and Catherine Dosterre, .	1691	M.L.	87
Varden, Thomas and Ellnor Charnley, ...	1634	M.L.	74
Vaughan, William and Mary Trench, ...	1722	M.L.	220
Verbren, Sarah and Charles Massoard, . . .	1768	M.L.	68
Varling, William and Elizabeth Farrell, . . .	1739	M.L.	94
Vernatil, John Mary (Rev.) and Sophia Magdalen De Sney,	1725	M.L.	161
Vessel, Margaret and John Grimion, ...	1781	M.L.	153
Vieare, Arabella and Edward La Caux, . . .	1729	M.L.	164
Vialla, Pauline and James de Favra, ...	1714	M.L.	19
Vigurs, Lucy and Michael Howstam, ...	1728	M.L.	55
Vila, John and Margaret Trinkey, ...	1791	M.L.	119
Villeneufve, Barmond and Antoinette Mullen, . .	1714	M.L.	20
Virrar, Anne and William White, ...	1727	M.L.	48
Vizard, Alice and George Smith, ...	1675	M.L.	11
Wade, Anne and Nathaniel Siakes, ...	1725	M.L.	12
„ John and Mary Carrol, widow, . . .	1741	M.L.	123
Wains, Francis and Mary Burton, widow, . . .	1730	M.L.	109
Wainwright, Peter and Sarah Hartson, . . .	1729	M.L.	85
Wakefield, George and Alice Karpen, ...	1673	M.L.	21
Wakely, Henrietta and Benjamin Everard, . .	1730	M.L.	191
Walker, Arthur and Ellnor Smith, ...	1732	M.L.	152
Walker, Hester (widow) and Rev. Samuel Scott, . .	1677	M.L.	86
„ Jane and John Whatlock, ...	1683	M.L.	49
„ John (Rev.) and Susannah Griswell, widow, .	1739	M.L.	143
„ John (Rev.) and Sarah Gutmet, widow, . .	1737	M.L.	179
„ Jonathan and Sarah Creagg, ...	1724	M.L.	61

CORRECTIONS, DUBLIN GRANT INDEX, 1272–1800—*continued.*

Name, Place, and Occupation.	Year.	Nature of Record.	Page.
Walker, Thomas (junior) and Jane Clark,	1741	M.L.	10
„ Thomas and Jane Gelmet,	1727	M.L.	8
Wall, Jane and Peter Gandy,	1676	M.L.	114
„ Mary and John Baldwin,	1731	M.L.	16
Waller, Elizabeth and James Depennmars,	1692	M.L.	61
„ Martha and Ralph Pitworth,	1741	M.L.	115
Wallis, James and Joyce Cawquick,	1678	M.L.	17
Walls, James and Sarah Growbly,	1680	M.L.	114
Walmsly, James and Mary Handleby,	1739	M.L.	10
Walsh, Catherine and John Richinson,	1733	M.L.	31
Walter, John and Elizabeth Good,	1775	M.L.	46
Walton, Samuel and Elizabeth Rowlandson,	1679	M.L.	1
Warburton, George and Elizabeth Trench,	1739	M.L.	119
Ward, Joan (widow) and William Braudy,	1715	M.L.	16
„ Margaret and John Church,	1740	M.L.	16
„ Richard and Elizabeth Short,	1676	M.L.	7
Werne, Hugh and Bridget Leaship,	1729	M.L.	11
Warren, Anne (widow) and Thomas Jolly,	1737	M.L.	101
„ James Peppard and Catherine Boniace,	1733	M.L.	19
Warrington, John and Dorothy Raper,	1679	M.L.	41
Watkins, Edward and Anne Ourlett,	1735	M.L.	109
Watson, James and Isabella Smith,	1741	M.L.	119
Watt, James and Anne Scott,	1722	M.L.	117
Wattars, Edward and Hester Eden,	1722	M.L.	1
Watton, Elizabeth and James Carlille,	1738	M.L.	19
Watts, Benjamin and Martha Boland,	1737	M.L.	6
Way, Elizabeth and Walter Chapland Bayly,	1708	M.L.	8
Wayle, Bernard and Elizabeth Cox, widow,	1689	M.L.	6
Webb, Edward and Margaret Bringly,	1671	M.L.	4
Webster, James and Margaret Ockvill,	1723	M.L.	99
Wedgworth, Denis and Elizabeth Geoghegan, widow,	1735	M.L.	8
Weeks, Philip and Anne Scarsfield,	1736	M.L.	99
Weir, James and Anne Kidd,	1733	M.L.	9
Weisley, Margaret and Herman Wentworth,	1679	M.L.	41
Weld, Nathaniel and Ann Thwaites,	1711	M.L.	115
„ Nathaniel and Elizabeth Tyrer,	1683	M.L.	6
Wellman, John and Mary Adams,	1708	M.L.	46
Wentworth, Herman and Margaret Weisley,	1679	M.L.	41
West, Jane and Thomas Brumloy,	1738	M.L.	119

CORRECTIONS, DUBLIN GRANT INDEX, 1272–1800—continued.

CONNEXIONS, DUBLIN GRANT INDEX, 1272-1800—*continued.*

Name, Place, and Occupation.	Year.	Nature of Record.	Page.
Williamson, Jane (widow) and Samuel Chandler,	1735	M.L.	
Willings, George and Isabella Juge,	1739	M.L.	
Willison, Nathan and Mary Tates,	1621	M L.	19
Wills, Anne and John Rowlett,	1724	M.L.	
„ Susannah and Ephraim Stewart,	1724	M.L.	
„ William and Frances Mitchel,	1729	M.L.	34
Willson, Susannah (widow) and Francis Omary,	1748	M.L.	
Wily, Jane and James Spence,	1683	M.L.	71
Winckworth, Mary and Sharington Grosvenor.	1676	M.L.	
Winter, Daniel and Martha White, widow,	1683	M.L.	6
Winterbotham, Benjamin and Sarah Larkey,	1737	M.L.	170
Withington, Joseph and Elinor Bennett,	1683	M.L.	
Wolfindon, Sarah and Thomas Rowell,	1736	M.L.	
Wolsely, Elizabeth and Edward Dowell,	1711	M.L.	
Woodle, Mary and Charles Bellew,	1729	M.L.	
Woodside, James and Jane Cordiner,	1731	M L.	
Worthy, Elizabeth (widow) and Marmaduke Foston,	1681	M.L.	34
Wotton, Peter and Mary Dillon,	1655	M.L.	9
Wright, John and Mary Campbel,	1705	M.L.	
Yates, Mary and Nathan Williams,	1684	M.L.	71
Yeates, Catherine (or Gates) and Dennis Dealy,	1746	M.L.	73
„ Grace (widow) and Gerald Canyam,	1729	M.L.	71
„ Isabella and John Chritchley,	1675	M.L.	
„ Jane and John Masters,	1681	M.L.	9
Young, Mary and John Hanbidge,	1711	M.L.	29
„ Sarah (widow) and Dennis George,	1735	M.L.	19
„ Thomas and Elinor Jones, widow,	1729	M L.	
Zackery, Mark and Jane Lloyd,	1682	M.L.	6

CORRECTIONS, DUBLIN GRANT INDEX, 1272–1800—*continued.*

The following entries in the Addenda to the Appendix of the
Twenty-sixth Report may be cancelled :--

Page	Lines to be Cancelled.
	Letter A.
943	Omit lines 1, 4, 6, 7, 8, 18, 19, 23, 31, 41, 43, 44, 44.
944	„ „ 2, 11, 17, 20, 23, 22, 34, 40, 43.
945	„ „ 7, 11, 16, 17, 18, 10, 21, 22, 41, 22, 27, 23, 38, 46, 47.
946	„ „ 6, 7, 12, 19, 22, 23, 23, 32, 44, 47, 30, 41, 47.
947	„ „ 7, 18, 20, 21, 22, 22, 23, 30, 71, 33, 20, 31, 23, 44, 40, 49, 30, 31.
948	„ „ 3, 13, 17, 18, 19.
	Letter B.
948	„ „ 1, 6, 9, 10, 11.
949	„ „ 1, 10, 14, 22, 20, 30, 33, 24, 33, 30, 30, 42, 44, 46, 46, 49, 51.
950	„ „ 6, 14, 17, 18, 20, 21, 29, 27, 30, 37, 46, 48.
951	„ „ 8, 10, 13, 17, 24, 20, 30, 34.
952	„ „ 2, 6, 14, 20, 21, 22, 30, 30, 44, 47, 46, 62.
953	„ „ 4, 12, 18, 22, 21, 22, 42, 47, 48.
954	„ „ 8, 16, 23, 42, 45, 40.
955	„ „ 2, 6, 14, 14, 18, 22, 24, 47, 30, 22, 31, 47, 48, 42.
956	„ „ 8, 11, 16, 17, 15, 20, 22, 24, 30, 40.
957	„ „ 2, 11, 15, 12, 19, 21, 30, 20, 25, 43, 46, 47.
958	„ „ 6, 16, 21, 24, 22, 34, 30, 30, 32, 44.
959	„ „ 3, 4, 5, 12, 44, 47, 42.
960	„ „ 11, 12, 13, 22, 24, 25, 27, 34, 44, 41, 62.
961	„ „ 1, 5, 6, 7, 8, 21, 22, 27, 12, 44, 47.
962	„ „ 16, 17, 22, 27, 30, 30, 40, 42.
963	„ „ 12, 14, 16, 17, 18, 22, 24, 25, 30, 20, 62.
964	„ „ 1, 7, 8, 11, 15, 16, 27, 25, 31, 37, 30, 44.
965	„ „ 2, 4, 7, 8, 11, 12, 42, 44, 41, 42.
966	„ „ 2, 6, 12, 14, 16, 24, 33, 44, 47, 30, 32.
967	„ „ 12.
	Letter C.
967	„ „ 3, 6, 16, 14, 22.
968	„ „ 1, 8, 17, 13, 18, 30, 21, 23, 26, 27, 44, 47, 42, 44, 42.
969	„ „ 4, 1, 22, 24, 22, 27, 44.
970	„ „ 1, 2, 3, 6, 8, 8, 11, 12, 16, 17, 22, 27, 23, 24, 24, 22, 44, 47, 62.

CORRECTIONS, DUBLIN GRANT INDEX, 1272–1800—*continued.*

Page.	Lines to be Cancelled.
	Letter C—*continued.*
971	Omit lines— 1, 2, 4, 5, 6, 8, 14, 16, 18, 19, 21, 23, 42, 45, 50, 51.
972	„ „ 4, 22, 24, 28.
973	„ „ 1, 4, 7, 28, 29, 34, 36, 44.
974	„ „ 12, 14, 19, 20, 22, 23, 26, 62, 53.
975	„ „ 5, 11, 12, 24, 41, 42, 47.
976	„ „ 1, 4, 9, 14, 19, 23, 27, 29, 32, 33, 38, 45, 52, 55, 51, 59.
977	„ „ 1, 3, 4, 8, 9, 10, 17, 20, 24, 25, 27, 35, 43, 44, 49.
978	„ „ 4, 8, 9, 21, 23, 30, 32, 34, 38, 50, 59, 62.
979	„ „ 1, 3, 14, 19, 20, 24, 26, 27, 29, 31, 32, 41.
980	„ „ 1, 3, 4, 8, 9, 12, 13.
	Letter D.
960	„ „ 2, 13, 24, 29, 27, 29, 31.
961	„ „ 19, 20, 21, 30, 41, 42.
962	„ „ 2, 4, 5, 6, 14, 24, 27, 34, 37, 47.
963	„ „ 19, 22, 41, 27, 30, 34, 38, 29, 44, 45, 47.
964	„ „ 22, 13, 14, 19, 21, 29, 34, 41.
965	„ „ 6, 14, 21, 29, 24, 33, 34, 35, 37, 28, 42, 49.
966	„ „ 2, 3, 8, 10, 11, 13, 14, 23, 30, 31, 33, 39, 41, 46.
967	„ „ 7, 28, 27, 43, 44, 49, 51.
968	„ „ 1, 2, 4, 6, 14, 29, 21, 29, 31.
	Letter E.
968	„ „ 1, 2, 2.
969	„ „ 2, 10, 11, 14, 19, 24, 15, 29, 34.
990	„ „ 2, 7, 20, 12, 20, 24, 29, 39, 31, 30, 42.
991	„ „ 2, 4, 7, 8, 29, 35, 32, 37, 38, 40, 51.
	Letter F.
992	„ „ 6, 11, 12, 14, 14, 16, 17, 19, 24, 79, 18, 22, 29, 34, 42, 44, 43.
993	„ „ 1, 2, 9, 17, 29, 34, 39, 41.
994	„ „ 16, 19, 22, 24, 27, 44, 49.
995	„ „ 2, 14, 24, 21, 29, 31, 39, 39, 44, 44, 49, 52.
996	„ „ 1, 4, 29, 22, 34, 41, 47, 51.
997	„ „ 5, 7, 9, 10, 21, 22, 29, 27, 22, 28, 45.
998	„ „ 2, 3, 4, 6, 11, 17, 21, 24, 24.

CORRECTIONS, DUBLIN GRANT INDEX, 1272–1800 —continued.

Page.	Lines to be Cancelled.

Letter G.

998	Omit lines 1, 6.
999	" " 13, 17, 31, 32, 33, 35, 36, 37, 49, 52.
1000	" " 2, 16, 33, 50, 52.
1001	" " 1, 2, 4, 14, 18, 22, 34, 35, 36, 37, 41, 42.
1002	" " 4, 10, 29, 22, 23, 24, 28, 31, 33, 34, 37, 41.
1003	" " 2, 4, 8, 10, 11, 14, 20, 22, 26, 34, 45, 48.
1004	" " 1, 8, 10, 18, 22, 23, 31, 33, 40, 41, 47, 48, 49, 44, 51.
1005	" " 1, 4, 5, 6, 10, 11, 14, 16, 17, 18, 21, 22, 23, 24, 27, 32.

Letter H.

1005	" " 2, 14, 16.
1006	" " 7, 21, 23, 32, 20, 36, 40, 42, 44.
1007	" " 6, 9, 13, 14, 23, 24, 27, 31, 32, 37, 41, 47, 49, 51.
1008	" " 1, 5, 9, 10, 14, 27, 33, 44, 49.
1009	" " 1, 5, 9, 13, 26, 29, 22, 33, 39, 46, 42, 46.
1010	" " 5, 6, 15, 17, 18, 28, 40, 46, 51.
1011	" " 8, 14, 22, 26, 28, 31, 34, 37, 40, 44, 48.
1012	" " 4, 5, 14, 18, 22, 23, 32, 33, 34, 46, 48, 50, 41, 52.
1013	" " 16, 23, 31, 29, 31, 45.
1014	" " 1, 6, 10, 11, 14, 14, 16, 20, 28, 32, 36, 37, 38, 41, 44, 47.
1015	" " 13, 14, 21, 22, 26, 23, 34, 44, 48, 42.
1016	" " 7, 10, 12, 28, 22, 28, 41, 47.
1017	" " 2.

Letter L.

1017	" " 4, 7, 8, 9, 16, 22, 24, 22, 34, 26.

Letter I.

1017	" " 1, 3, 12, 23.
1018	" " 2, 4, 11, 16, 25, 32, 34, 38.
1019	" " 4, 23, 30, 43, 45.
1020	" " 1, 11, 16, 22, 38, 52.
1021	" " 2.

CORRECTIONS, DUBLIN GRANT INDEX, 1272–1800—*continued*.

Page.	Lines to be Cancelled.

Letter K.

1021	Omit lines 1, 2, 6, 7, 9, 14, 14, 22, 29, 35, 37, 38, 39, 42, 44.
1022	„ „ 21, 27, 32, 33, 43, 43, 60.
1023	„ „ 4, 7, 8, 14, 16, 22, 24, 25, 32.
1024	„ „ 8, 27.

Letter L.

1024	„ „ 8.
1025	„ „ 1, 22, 32, 34, 36, 38, 52, 45, 44, 62.
1026	„ „ 8, 4, 6, 12, 18, 19, 22, 26, 32, 32, 32, 48, 16.
1027	„ „ 11, 16, 18, 19, 22, 26, 22, 32, 34, 32, 44, 47.
1028	„ „ 7, 12, 14, 22.
1029	„ „ 8, 7, 12, 14, 14, 16, 16, 17, 22, 29, 42.
1030	„ „ 9, 14, 17, 12, 21, 22, 22, 32, 37, 41.

Letter M.

1031	„ „ 1, 7, 8, 17, 18, 20, 21, 22, 42.
1032	„ „ 1, 7, 8, 14, 16, 24, 22, 22, 22, 27, 42, 42.
1033	„ „ 1, 18, 22, 27, 16, 42, 17, 22, 22, 22.
1034	„ „ 3, 6, 7, 21, 22, 22, 22, 22.
1035	„ „ 1, 4, 8, 12, 14, 16, 12, 27, 22, 22, 40.
1036	„ „ 4, 6, 7, 16, 12, 21, 22, 27, 22, 31, 22, 41, 42, 47, 42.
1037	„ „ 4, 9, 12, 17, 12, 21, 27, 16, 41, 42, 52.
1038	„ „ 12, 14, 22, 22, 22, 24, 31, 32, 41, 14, 16, 12.
1039	„ „ 7, 2, 6, 17, 20, 21, 22, 27, 22, 14, 18, 12.
1040	„ „ 1, 17, 12, 18, 22, 21, 22, 22, 22, 27, 26, 46, 52.
1041	„ „ 1, 2, 8, 16, 12, 14, 22, 22, 22, 22.

Letter N.

1041	„ „ 7, 10, 11, 12.
1042	„ „ 12, 14, 12, 22, 31, 31, 32, 41.
1043	„ „ 8, 16, 17, 31, 22, 22.
1044	„ „ 7, 8, 14.

Letter O.

1044	„ „ 1, 3, 16, 22, 22, 22, 24, 22, 22, 37.
1045	„ „ 7, 20, 22, 21, 22, 27, 27.

CORRECTIONS, DUBLIN GRANT INDEX, 1272–1800—*continued.*

Page.	Lines to be Cancelled.
	Letter P.
1045	Omit line 7.
1046	„ „ 4, 9, 16, 19, 21, 41, 45, 48, 51.
1047	„ „ 1, 3, 5, 6, 10, 14, 17, 29, 34, 41, 45, 49, 51.
1048	„ „ 5, 6, 9, 10, 16, 20, 21, 23, 26, 62, 36, 50, 61
1049	„ „ 1, 4, 12, 14, 15, 25, 27, 54, 46, 41, 44, 49, 51.
1050	„ „ 4, 13, 34, 53, 41, 45.
1051	„ „ 3, 12, 14, 16, 19, 20, 45, 34, 46, 56, 56, 51.
1052	„ „ 3, 4.
	Letter Q.
1053	„ „ 1, 4, 9, 13, 14, 45, 46.
	Letter R.
1054	„ „ 4, 9.
1055	„ „ 3, 9, 16, 19, 21, 12, 24, 49, 43, 29, 34, 45, 46, 47.
1056	„ „ 1, 3, 2, 4, 5, 9, 14, 17, 29, 42, 43.
1057	„ „ 5, 4, 14, 29, 34, 41.
1058	„ „ 4, 6, 7, 9, 25, 29, 39, 43, 14, 49.
1059	„ „ 3, 14, 16, 30, 39, 49, 40, 43, 44, 46.
1060	„ „ 3, 7, 6, 10, 14, 16, 41, 47, 34, 46, 44.
	Letter S.
1059	„ „ 14, 21, 34, 36, 49, 31, 46.
1060	„ „ 3, 30, 37, 41, 43.
1061	„ „ 1, 4, 6, 11, 14, 17, 16, 49, 21, 40, 34, 39, 40, 41
1062	„ „ 31, 57, 49, 61.
1063	„ „ 3, 6, 14, 16, 49, 34, 33, 49, 49, 13
1064	„ „ 9, 14, 24, 32, 35, 39, 41, 43, 43.
1065	„ „ 4, 9, 14, 49, 51, 34, 49, 31, 37.
1066	„ „ 14, 24, 17, 49.
1067	„ „ 4, 12, 14, 16, 17, 49, 39, 31, 39, 46, 43, 14
1068	„ „ 7, 9, 14, 34, 49, 49, 33, 34, 49, 44, 46, 47.
1069	„ „ 3, 7, 12, 49, 49, 49, 41, 49, 46, 41.
1070	„ „ 3, 9, 13, 34, 39, 36, 39, 39, 43.

CORRECTIONS, DUBLIN GRANT INDEX, 1272–1800—*continued*.

Page.	Lines to be Cancelled.

Letter T.

1071	Omit lines 2, 7, 12, 17, 21, 22, 24, 34, 38, 42, 51.
1072	6, 12, 17, 25, 27, 42, 52.
1073	4, 6, 22, 34, 38, 40, 41, 42.
1074	4, 12, 24, 34, 38, 47, 41, 42.
1075	4, 8, 11, 13, 14, 18, 21, 22, 24, 17, 28, 21, 27, 47, 47.
1076	8, 10, 12, 14.

Letter U.

1076	4, 5.

Letter V.

1076	1, 7.
1077	3, 6, 11, 10, 17, 18, 19, 23, 26, 31, 31, 36, 33, 47, 40.

Letter W.

1078	2, 9, 11, 12, 14, 17, 24, 27, 34, 39, 41.
1079	13, 14, 16, 23, 24, 26, 27, 41, 51, 62.
1080	6, 23, 24, 40, 52.
1081	2, 11, 22, 34.
1082	1, 3, 6, 7, 8, 12, 20, 24, 27, 28, 31, 27, 32, 41, 42, 41, 44, 47.
1083	2, 12, 14, 21, 22, 26, 32, 24, 26, 47.
1084	2, 4, 10, 20, 22, 20, 31, 26, 27, 12, 22
1085	1, 2, 4, 6, 12, 14, 20, 22, 23, 25, 30, 22, 42, 42, 46.
1086	42, 27, 28, 24, 37, 28, 61.
1087	27, 34, 46.
1088	3, 6, 14, 21, 40.
1089	1, 12.

Letter Y.

1089	3, 6, 7, 8, 12, 17, 12

APPENDIX II.

Extract from Memorandum by Mr. James Mills on the Departmental Letters and Official Papers, 1760-1780, transferred in 1808.

Among the matters illustrated by this collection may be noted the progress of the Bills of the Irish Parliament, which may be traced in the papers under the heads of Parliament, Council Office, Ireland, Irish Office, and Council Office, London, and sometimes under Treasury and Home Office. A curious example of the way in which Bills of consequence were sometimes pushed through the necessary stages is given in the following letter of the Under Secretary at the Irish Office in London (Irish Office letter, 1776, April 21):

"Crown-street [London], April 21, 1776.

"Sir,—Two days since, I called on Sr. Stanier Porten to settle the manner of transmitting the Bills; and as it was determined to send them by a messenger, I gave notice thereof to the Council officers, and as all the persons concern'd in forwarding the business seem to have been animated with an uncommon zeal for dispatch, I think some of the particulars not unworthy to come to his Excellency's knowledge.

"Mr. Frewen, the Deputy Clerk of the Crown, obtain'd the Lord High Steward's permission to leave his attendance on him in the Hall,* that he might examine the Bills with the transcripts, but the Attorney-General's clerk, who is the constant coadjutor to that officer on these occasions, could not possibly quit his station; therefore Mr. Dring, of the Council Office, acted as his deputy, and before the Lords had adjourn'd, which was about six o'clock, the examination of the Bills was finish'd.

"Sr. Stanier Porten, whose curiosity had carried him to the trial, left the Hall at 2 o'clock, to get the proclamation sign'd by the King, which he got done.

"Mr. Cotterel was obliged to attend on the Foreign Ambassadors in the Hall during the whole trial; but has found time to write to you what the messenger brings with him, and to give some directions, ordering the messenger to attend at 10 o'clock.

"In the meantime Mr. Dring was to get the Bills sign'd and seal'd.

"Accordingly, he went to Mr. Rigby's, where my Lord President and the Attorney-General were to dine, but was refused to be admitted. Upon this he went back to the office, wrote a letter in the name of Mr. Cotterel to Lord President, requesting him to prevail on the Attorney-General to sign the Bills, for which purpose, he said, a clerk was waiting with them. These he carried in his bag, and Mr. Rigby's servants condescending to give the letter to Lord President, in 10 minutes the Attorney-General sign'd them, and dispatch'd him. Then he proceeded to the Lord High Steward's, who was to dine at 8 o'clock, and getting there a little before, got the seal affixt; and by half-past 9 they were made up and deliver'd to Haworth, the messenger, who inform'd me that he should not sett off that night (all this was between 2 and 10 o'clock yesterday), as a messenger was come from Dublin, and Lord Weymouth must answer some letters, which he could not do till this day.

" Now I must observe, that so many great and little people, who were all concern'd to complete and perfect the business so necessary at this time for the Irish Government, concurring to act their several parts, at a time they really might have been excused (if they had not been well disposed) almost deserves a chronicle; though I own it puzzles me in some degree that it should have so happen'd.

" You will be so good as to acquaint his Excellency with the purport hereof, and believe me to be,

" Dear Sir,

" Your very faithfull and obedient humble Servant,

" ROBT. WESTON."

The discussion in London between representatives of the Irish Government and the London authorities on the laws affecting Irish Trade is reported in a number of very full letters written by Sackville Hamilton, one of the Irish representatives, to the Chief Secretary (Trade, 1780, Jan. 1 to April 11). Hamilton met with every consideration, and speaks with much satisfaction of Lord North's " Honor, Steadiness, and Favor for Ireland." (Feb. 3.)

Under the head " POST OFFICE " are some interesting papers describing the mode in which the mails were conveyed through the country. Almost to the end of the period covered by this collection, the mails were carried by a mounted postboy riding alone. It is no marvel that they were frequently robbed.

Robbers, however, were not the only danger that the postboys had to face, as may be seen from the following letter :—

" SIR,—I am commanded by Lord Clermont to represent to you, for the information of his Excellency the Lord Lieutenant, that on Wednesday morning the 1st inst. between 1 and 3 o'clock, the centinels at Newgate stopped the postboy who was carrying the mail from this office to Kilcullen, and one of them struck the horse with his musquet, and the other stabbed him in two places in the side with his bayonet, so that he is still dangerously ill.

" I am to add that about six in the morning of Monday, the 6th inst. while it was full daylight, a centinel at Newgate struck another postboy who was bringing the mail from Kilcullen to this office, and wounded him twice in the head with his gun.

" The 55th Regiment was upon guard on the 1st inst., and the 47th on the 6th.

" As the safe and speedy conveyance of His Majesty's Mails is of the utmost consequence to the trade and correspondence of this Kingdom, which, together with the persons employed in the service, have always been under the protection of Government, Lord Clermont thinks himself oblig'd to beg His Excellency will be pleas'd to issue his orders that the mails may not in future be detain'd by the soldiers upon guard, that the postboys may not be molested, that the offenders I have mentioned may be punish'd in an exemplary manner, to deter others from the like attempts, and that the Postmaster of Kilcullen may have satisfaction for the damage done to his horse, or the loss of him if he dies.

"It would be injustice not to acknowledge that the commanding officers of the 55th and 47th Regiments have behaved themselves with great civility and politeness upon this unlucky occasion. They with all diligence discovered the offenders, and offered to try them by a court martial, but as Lord Clermont was then in the country, and expected in town in a few days I thought it right to wait for his lordship's orders.

"I have the honour to be with great respect,

"Sir,

"Your most obedient and most faithful

humble servant,

"JOHN WILSON, Sec.

"Gen¹. Post Office, Dublin,

"Aug⁵. 14th, 1770."

It was not, however, until 1788 that the merchants of Cork and Belfast began to agitate for a more secure and convenient mode of conveying the mails. The first effort in this direction is to be found in an offer made by three merchants of Cork in the following letter:—

"Cork, 3rd Sep⁰., 1785.

"MY LORD AND SIR,—As his Majesties Post Masters General of this Kingdom we take the liberty of addressing you, humbly to submit to your consideration a plan for conveying the mail to and from Dublin hither in post carriages, agreeable to the mode now so universally adopted thro'out England. We are well aware of the many difficulties we have to encounter in venturing upon so very new and hazardous an undertaking, yet so ambitious are we to promote what most be of such utility to trade and general advantage to the kingdom, that, under y⁰ hon⁰ˡᵉ patronage, we are ready to give ample security for establishing regular post carriages and horses, which during the six summer months shall take up and bring down the mail in 28 hours, and in winter not exceed 30 hours; allowing us at the rate of Mr. Palmer's* original engagement, which we understand to be 3d. per English mile down and 1½d. back, with half a guinea p. week to each of the attending guards (should such be deem'd necessary), warranting us a contract for twenty-one years or any longer engagement you may deem our humble endeavours worthy of.

"We have the honor to remain with the greatest respect,

"My Lord and Sir,

"Your most humble and obed⁰. serv⁰,

"H. O'DONNOGHUE,

"JOHN ANDERSON,

"H⁰. FORTESCUE.

"R⁰ Hon⁰ˡᵉ the Post Masters General."

* Mail coach contractor in England.

This proposal was favourably received by the Post Office authorities in Dublin, and it was recommended by them in a letter from the Secretary of 7th September, 1785. They considered that "very essential advantages must result, not only by the more speedy conveyance of His Majesty's mails, but from the communication which will thereby be opened in little more than twenty-four hours between Dublin and Corke, which, by the present mode of travelling, takes up a space of five days."

Further consideration showed difficulties which prevented the immediate carrying out of this improvement. In a letter of 13th December, 1786, the Secretary writes:— "Upon enquiry into the state of the roads throughout the Kingdom in general, they appear'd to be in such a situation as to preclude the possibility of such an establishment at present, nor was it likely that they would be so soon put into so serious a repair for that purpose as might be wish'd. That the moment they were so, and that contractors could be found to undertake such a plan, they would again call the attention of Government to that very important and desirable object."

In 1788 a more than usually important mail robbery brought the question again into prominence.

"Gen. Post Office, Dublin,

"Thursday, Feb. 28th, 1788.

"Information is further received this morning that the postboy with the mail for Dublin was again robbed last night at nine o'clock, between Dunleer and Drogheda, by two men, one a tall, the other a short man. The latter of whom tied the postboy's hands behind his back with a garter, and took the entire mail away, containing the postbags from the following towns that should have arrived here this morning, viz., Armagh, Banbridge, Belfast, Castlebellingham, Draghsdea, Drogore, Dundalk, Dungannon, Dunleer, Flurrybridge, Hillsborough, Loughbrickland, Lurganbreen, Markethill, Newry, Newtownards. * * * *"

This robbery appears to have hastened the action of the authorities, and in the following month an advertisement was published for proposals for "carrying the mails in coaches, attended by guards." In considering the cost of the new arrangements, the Postmasters-General observe (letter, 31 May, 1789)—"That as the solicitor's bills for the expence of prosecutions for mail robberies since the establishment of this Office amount, upon an average, to £1,000 a year, a saving nearly to that amount may be expected to the revenue of this Office if the Mail Coach plan shall be established."

Smugglers plied their calling with much success, notwithstanding the Irish Fleet of Revenue Cruisers. Several letters point to the little port of Rush, though so near Dublin, as one of the most formidable homes of the smuggler. During war, especially the American War, the smugglers were frequently found manning and directing the French and American privateers, which infested the coast and seriously injured the trade of the country. The following letter, preserved under head of Revenue, illustrates how completely the trade was sometimes at their mercy :—

"Custom House, Waterford,
"13th August, 1781.

"HONOURED SIRS, I am sorry to acquaint your Hons. that this port is now so compleatly block'd up by privateers that no vessel going out, or coming in, can possibly escape; one of them, a lugger of 16 six-pounders, commanded by Dowling, just now chaced the Hunter Impress boat into the very harbour; this privateer lies at anchor frequently in the sound between the two Salters, and slips out occasionally on seeing any ship. A brig and lugger chased several vessels yesterday (Sunday) off the Tower, and took one of our coal traders (the Iris, Capn. Tedball) and two sloops of little value, one of which they ransomed for one hundred guineas, and the other they suffer'd to pass free, but finding the Iris had a few packs of hay yarn on board, which she took in here, they would not ransom her on any account. Another of the privateers, which has committed great depredations on this coast, carrys 26 nine and twelve-pounders and 250 men, and has (it is reported by some who were prisoners on board her) ransoms on board, to the amount of forty thousand pounds; she is call'd the Princess de Norrice, one McCarthy, commander; there is also another cutter on the coast, call'd the Chardon, of 20 guns. In short, I can assure your Hons. with certainty, that scarce a day passes that vessels are not taken in view of the people about Dunmore and Tramore, and unless some effectual steps shall be taken to prevent it, there must be an end to all trade here, as insurance will not be had for any premium. And what makes our situation the more deplorable is that the Nemesis, frigate, and Viper, cutter, have been order'd for Cork, whither they sail'd the 10th inst, to convoy a fleet from thence to England, so that we have now a repetition of every evil to expect from those pirates, who were hardly enough to take many vessels at the harbour's mouth, at a time when they knew that some of his Majesty's ships of war were at anchor within.

"I am, with great respect, Houd. Sirs,
"Your most obedt. hble. servt.,
"J. GAHAN,
"Surv."

Great as was the danger from the privateer pirates, the unlighted coast formed a still graver source of disaster. Some interesting particulars are included under the head of "Light Houses," especially as to those at Hook, Tuskar, and Howth. So late as 1788 the question whether oil lamps might not be an improvement on the open coal fires hitherto used, was under discussion; experiments were gravely made and reported on.

Among matters of internal interest, the occasional distress caused by general or local failures of the crops, at several times occupied the attention of Government. Among the means adopted were encouragement of coastwise conveyances of corn from districts of plenty to distressed districts, purchase of corn to be retailed at low price to the poor, &c.

A letter of Lord Temple, when leaving office, to his successor, Lord Northington ("Lord Lieutenant," 23 May, 1783), deals very fully with the means of meeting the then threatened dearth. Among other measures referred to, he adds that "the laws of this Kingdom do not enable Government to stop the distillery, else an immediate relief might be afforded against the threatened calamity."

The Excise authorities had already (Revenue, 19 July, 1766) called attention to the waste of corn from unchecked distilling in time of scarcity, and had urged this an additional reason for increased aid from the military for their officers.

Section 6 of the Act 21 & 22 Geo. III. c. 34, which enabled Catholic priests to register themselves, has led to the preservation of lists of the Catholic clergy of several dioceses. Some of these registers are very full of interesting details, including, beside the name and rank of the clergyman, his age, and the date and place of receiving the different orders, and the names of the ordaining bishops.

Under the head, "Surveys," are some very interesting letters of Colonel Vallancey, describing the accident by which he discovered Petty's maps in the Royal Library in Paris, and his subsequent progress in the transcription of the maps. Two of these letters are subjoined:—

"MY LORD,—Having by accident turned over the King's Catalogue of the Bibliotheque Royal de France, a discovery offered of much importance to Ireland. On enquiry of Lord Erisfort, the Secretary of State, &c., I believe your Grace will find that the Down Survey or the survey of the forfeited estates, made by Sir Wm. Petty, are frequently allowed to be evidence in Court, in cases of property. That on this account an office called the Surveyor General's of Land, was established for the preservation of this survey; that many years since, a fire in the Castle of Dublin consumed many of these surveys; that the copy in possession of Lord Shelburn is imperfect, and cannot supply this defect. That these copies are all laid down on a scale too small for ascertaining the just bounds of estates, and were not intended by Sir Wm. Petty for that purpose, but only a contraction of the great originals towards making a small map of Ireland.

"That the original on a large scale was shipped for England, in order to be engraved in London, in the reign of Queen Ann; the ship was taken in the passage by a French privateer and carried into St. Malos, and many fruitless searches have been made to recover these Surveys.

"Lord Harcourt made every enquiry possible for them in France; Lord Shelburn did the same; the Catalogues of the French Libraries were turned to in vain; no such maps appearing in the Catalogues under the words Cartes or MSS, the Librarians never gave themselves farther trouble. I have experienced the same both at Oxford and Cambridge.

"My pursuits this day in the French King's Catalogue were for old Copies of the Bible, and consequently turned to the volume entitled Theology, curious to know in what manner the collection was made. I perused the Preface, and to my great astonishment at page 50, found the enclosed account of the original Survey of Ireland, by Sir Wm. Petty, on the large scale, and I suppose complete; if not, probably those remain those now deficient in the Surveyor General's Office.

"If on enquiry your Grace shall find these to be of consequence and worthy of being obtained, or of being copied, there can be no doubt of its being accomplished, by application of Lord Sydney or of Mr. Pitt to the French Ambassador.

"Disappointed of the opportunity of dedicating my map of Ireland to your Grace, which I had hopes of doing in the most superb manner the art of engraving would permit, and desirous of throwing my mite into the great Pyramid of popularity, so justly erected to your Grace's memory in Ireland, I take the liberty of communicating this discovery to your Grace, and if it should happen that copies may at length be taken of the originals now in the French King's Library, that your Grace will be pleased to have in memory the employment of my eldest son, an excellent Engineer and Draughtsman, who after serving all the American War, is now starving on half pay at St. Omers.

"I have the honour to be with most perfect respect,

"Your Grace's most obedient most humble Servant,

"CHAS. VALLANCEY.

"Cecil Street, 27th Jan., 1786.

"His Grace the D. of Rutland."

"Paris, 4th March, 1787.

SIR.—I have the honour to acquaint you that I was dispatched by Lord Sydney on the 21st ulto., and arrived here on the 26th, on the next day had an audience of the Duke of Dorset, who furnished me with a letter to Monsr. Le Noire, Chief Librarian. This gentleman was in the country and did not arrive till this day. Monsr. Le Noire has assured me of every means to facilitate the copy of the maps; it must be made in the library, he said we might work from nine in the morning to six at evening. This would be sufficient; but the under librarian objects to three hours and declares he will shut up the library each day at twelve. I requested M. Le Noire to permit the books to be taken to my lodgings; he said, the King's orders were positive against such an indulgence, but the under librarian whispered it would be granted if the D. of Dorset would ask it of the King. In vain I solicited for a sight of the maps, on my first arrival. The sub-librarian could not grant that favour till M. Le Noire arrived—he had indeed shewn them to Baron Power, but I must wait for an order. At length he granted me that favour yesterday, for two minutes only. At the first cast of my eye, they appear to be the maps of each barony, with the Down Survey, only as far as it extended in each barony; executed in a more masterly manner than anything of the kind remaining in Ireland. The title page is finely illuminated, and every part shows great care and attention has been paid to this work.

"It is impossible to form an idea of the time it will require to make this copy: the shortest will be four months from this date; three will be sufficient if I am indulged to take the books to my lodgings, which are within pistol shot of the library, in hopes the proximity might be some inducement to this favour; but, if the under librarian carries his point of granting me only three hours in the day to work, it will require much longer time than I have specified. Thus circumstanced in the midst of the most expensive city of the world, even for common necessaries of life, I hope, sir, you will be pleased to send me a further credit, more than half the sum advanced, being already expended.

"I have the honour to be, sir, with perfect respect,

"Your most obedient, most humble Servant,

"CHARLES VALLANCEY.

"Address—

"Hotel des Etats Unies,

"Rue de Gaillon.

"Rt. Hon. Mr. Orde, &c., &c., &c."

Perhaps the latest instance of the warlike use of a rath is contained in a letter describing a forcible resistance to the Sheriff of County of Tipperary at Oldcastle, seven miles from Templemore. "The Garrison, as it was called, was a Danish Fort. the form circular, and planted with fir trees that made the place so dark as not to be able to see into it; the banks round it were about eighteen feet high, with a stake hedge at top and a deep loose round this, in an open field on a rising ground." So strong was the place that Sir John Cayden, the writer of the letter, and the Sheriff agreed that it could not be taken without artillery.

The humane desire to improve the condition of the prisons, which was being urged on by Howard, led to inquiries and much beneficial work in Ireland. Towards the end of this period Sir Jeremiah FitzPatrick, M.D., was appointed Inspector-General of Prisons and Hospitals. The following account of the difficulties he met in attempting to introduce reforms in the Marshalsea, is of interest:—

"To His Excellency, George Nugent Grenville Temple, Lord Lieutenant-General and General Governor of Ireland.

"The Memorial of Sir Jeremiah FitzPatrick, Inspector-General of Prisons,

"Most Humbly Showeth—

"That in consequence of the rules proposed for the effectual regulation of the Four Courts Marshalsea, agreeable to your Excellency's will, the greatest disorder and violence has taken place in that prison; in so much, that Memorialist is in the greatest danger of his life, and finds that without your Excellency's protection he cannot with safety visit that Marshalsea again, not even to have the works at present undertaken finished.

"By the regulations, the Marshal considers himself injured in point of expence. The wealthy, who have families lodged with them for several years past—and still remain, altho' entitled to the two last Insolvent Acts—but will not give up their effects to their just creditors; those who have more than one room; those who keep mistresses, and all the whisky drinkers, are disobliged; so that in place of your Memorialist finding friends, after all his exertions for prisoners—it was with the greatest difficulty he escaped their rage on Fryday morning last—which he effected by sliding thro' the hatches, when they least expected it.

"On Saturday Memorialist received the enclosed card, dated the 21st, and on Sunday was continued by a Member of Parliament, and other gentlemen not to venture there again without the army or some person to protect Memorialist.

"On Monday Memorialist received the note dated the 23rd June. Your Memorialist, however, was determined not to become troublesome to Government, except it became unavoidable, and conscious that he was discharging his duty in fulfilling your Excellency's commands, he went yesterday to see the works in respect to the Bath and Hospitals, &c., carried into effect; and prepared himself with pistols, which he had in his coat-pockets, with a large coat thrown over his shoulders, loosely. Memorialist had not been one minute in the yard, when one of the prisoners, by whom he had formerly been abused, accused him by saying the bathing would soon be begun; alluding in Memorialist's opinion, to the pumping. Memorialist went on to give his directions to the men who were at work at the bath, and finding himself followed by near one hundred persons, and that a prisoner who personated a judge in old robes, with a person before him who kept beating an old tin vessel (as if a drum) paraded the yard, and that numbers wore cunning round Memorialist, he began to entertain fears for his safety, and was moving towards an open space to avoid them, and sometimes looking towards the upper windows, from whence he heard they would fire. Memorialist foot struck against some obstacle, on which one of the pistols, until then concealed, went off, and as the muzzle was upwards, fired into the air. Memorialist immediately, but with difficulty escaped, which he verily believes he could not have done had he not kept another loaded pistol presented whilst he retreated to the door.

"Memorialist was particularly abused by three or four persons, who seemed the ringleaders, and by a William Alexander English, who vehemently swore that Memorialist was acting officiously, and had no right to visit or inspect that Marshalsea; and that if Memorialist ever attempted to enter his apartment for the purpose of carrying the proposed or any other regulation into execution, that he would kick Memorialist downstairs, no matter by whom directed or supported.

"Your Memorialist declares that he is thus prevented from discharging the duties of his office, and of forwarding the regulations so humanely intended by your Excellency, therefore prays protection.

"June the 24, 1788."

The following copy of the draft of a reply to a Treasury letter gives an explanation of a very confusing use of one of the terms employed to describe the money of account here. It throws light on a question which even yet sometimes causes a difficulty.

"Dublin Castle, 16th February, 1786.

"Dear Sir,—Agreeably to your desire I communicated the enclosed petition of Charlotte, Duchess Dowager of Athol, to my Lord Lieutenant, and His Grace requests that you will inform Mr. Pitt that the expression in His Majesty's grant for the payment of Her Grace's annuity in lawful money of Great Britain does not imply British currency distinguished from Irish currency, with a difference of exchange, but means no more than that the payment of the annuity shall be made in such lawful money as is current in Great Britain as well as in Ireland. The expression is made use of in similar grants and is common in bonds and other legal proceedings here where Irish money only is the consideration.

"Your most faithful and obedient servant,

"T. O[rde].

"George Rose, Esq."

I have not touched on the letters of political consequence, yet the collection contains many such. These are ranged chiefly under the heads of Home Office, Lord Lieutenant, and Treasury. Among these are to be found, besides official letters of advice and direction from the Government in London, in many cases also the original drafts of the replies, which show not only the answer sent but sometimes the manner in which, after repeated changes, the ultimate form of the answer was arrived at. The whole collection forms an important addition to the now available sources of the history of Ireland in the last century.